AMERICAN TROUBLEMAKERS

Mother Jones: Labor Crusader

T★AMERICAN★S ROUBLEMAKERS

Titles in Series

AMERICAN TROUBLEMAKERS

MOTHER JONES:
Labor Crusader

Joan C. Hawxhurst

With an Introduction by James P. Shenton

RSVP

RAINTREE
STECK-VAUGHN
PUBLISHERS
The Steck-Vaughn Company

Austin, Texas

In memory of another fiery white-haired lady who had faith,
Martha Sell Hawxhurst, 1905–1991.
"Pray for the dead and fight like hell for the living!" —Mother Jones

CONSULTANTS

Elizabeth Blackmar
Associate Professor of HIstory
Department of History
Columbia College
New York, New York

Robert M. Goldberg
Consultant to the Social Studies
 Department
(former Department Chair)
Oceanside Middle School
Oceanside, New York

MANAGING EDITOR
Richard G. Gallin

PROJECT MANAGER
Julie Klaus

PHOTO EDITOR
Margie Foster

A Gallin House Press Book

Library of Congress Cataloging-in-Publication Data
Hawxhurst, Joan C.
    Mother Jones / written by Joan C. Hawxhurst.
        p.   cm. — (American Troublemakers)
    "A Gallin House Press Book."—T.p. verso
    Includes bibliographical references and index.
    Summary: Describes the life of the American labor organizer
Mary Harris Jones.
    ISBN 0-8114-2327-1
    1. Jones, Mother, 1843?-1930 — Juvenile literature.   2. Labor
leaders — United States — Biography — Juvenile literature.   3. Women
in trade-unions —United States — Biography — Juvenile literature.
4. Trade-unions — United States — Organizing — History — Juvenile
literature.   [1. Jones, Mother, 1843?-1930.   2. Labor leaders.]
I.Title.   II. Series.
HD8073.J6h39   1994
331.88' 092—dc20
[B]   92-22191
                                                                       CIP
                                                                        AC

Printed and bound in the United States

1 2 3 4 5 6 7 8 9 0   LB   98 97 96 95 94 93

CONTENTS

Map

Mary Harris Jones (Mother Jones)

INTRODUCTION

by James P. Shenton

$\mathbb{B}$iography is the history of the individual lives of men and women. In all lives, there is a sequence that begins with birth, evolves into the development of character in childhood and adolescence, is followed by the emergence of maturity in adulthood, and finally concludes with death. All lives follow this pattern, although with each emerge the differences that make each life unique. These distinctive characteristics are usually determined by the particular area in which a person has been most active. An artist draws his or her specific identity from the area of the arts in which he or she has been most active. So the writer becomes an author; the musician, a performer or composer; the politician, a senator, governor, president, or statesperson. The intellectual discipline to which one is attached identifies the scientist, historian, economist, literary critic, or political scientist, among many. Some aspects of human behavior are identified as heroic, cowardly, corrupt, or just ordinary. The task of the biographer is to explain why a particular life is worth remembering. And if the effort is successful, the reader draws from it insights into a vast range of behavior patterns. In a sense, biography provides lessons from life.

Some lives become important because of the position a person holds. Typical would be that of a U.S. President in which a biographer compares the various incumbents to determine their comparative importance. Without question, Abraham Lincoln was a profoundly significant President, much more so than Warren G. Harding whose administration was swamped by corruption. Others achieve importance because of their role in a particular area. So Emily Dickinson and Carl Sandburg are recognized as important poets and Albert Einstein as a great scientist.

Implicit in the choice of biographical subjects is the idea that each somehow affected history. Their lives explain something about the world in which they lived, even as they affect our lives and those of generations to come. But there is another considera-

7

tion: Some lives are more interesting than those of others. Within each life is a great story that illuminates human behavior.

Then there are those people who are troublemakers, people whom we cannot ignore. They are the people who both upset and fascinate us. Their singular quality is that they are uniquely different. Troublemakers are irritating, perhaps frightening, frustrating, and disturbing, but never dull. They march to their own drummer, and they are original.

In the 19th century, it was not normally assumed that an aging woman would begin a new career and that it would make her name a household word—even more unlikely that she would become a major labor leader. Whatever the expectation, that is what happened to Mary Harris, who was born in Ireland in about 1830 and who died in 1930 in Maryland. Married in 1861 to George Jones in Tennessee, she lost him and their children in 1867 to a yellow fever epidemic. Widowed and childless at 37, she moved to Chicago.

Profoundly committed to workers and their families, she dedicated her life to improving their lives. Her early career as a schoolteacher had given her the confidence and ability to speak before large groups of people in direct and simple language. She understood the needs of ordinary people. When she spoke, they recognized her as one of their own. It was an identification strengthened by her willingness to share their lives. When the Knights of Labor asked her to work with striking coal miners, she quickly agreed. The misery and hard life of the mining camps deepened her instinctive sympathy for the poor. Among miners a legend soon spread of a white-haired woman ready to fight to change their lives for the better. Coal miners and their families christened her "Mother Jones."

Wherever workers needed help, she was there. It was not enough to hear of conditions within coal mines or child labor in Alabama cotton textile factories; she went into the mines and factories to see for herself. No audience listening to her pungent descriptions of harsh working conditions was left indifferent. Her home was wherever workers struggled for their rights. When their courage flagged, she rallied them to refuse to bow to threats or flinch from danger. Her commanding but nurturing presence provided a model of how to deal with life's struggles. Unsurprisingly, her memory still lives wherever workers claim their rights.

CHAPTER ONE

A Little Irish Girl Becomes a Teacher

W hen Mary Harris was born more than 150 years ago no one knew that she would someday be called "the most dangerous woman in America." Back then she was just another baby born of poor Irish farmers. Today no one knows exactly when she was born. There are very few old records of births left today in her home country of Ireland, and she gave different birth dates at different points in her life. It seems that as she got older, she kept giving earlier birth dates. By the time she died in 1930, she had set her birthday 100 years earlier, on May 1, 1830.

Centuries before a little Irish girl named Mary Harris was born, Ireland had been conquered by the British. In 1801, Ireland became part of the United Kingdom. Many Irish peasant farmers no longer owned the land. Instead, they were forced to rent houses and land from wealthy British landlords. The Irish Catholic peasants were expected to grow grain such as wheat in order to pay their rents. The British Protestant landlords exported the grain from Ireland. Because the peasants had to give most of their farm produce to the landlords for rent, they had only a little for themselves. British landlords who wanted to make more money from their land either raised the Irish farmers' rents or turned farmland into pasture for cattle. When they could not afford the increased rents, many Irish peasants were evicted and found themselves without food or a place to live. The Irish countryside was crowded with peasants who were desperately poor and hungry.

The Irish peasants grew very angry at the landlords who had taken everything from them, and mass rebellions sprang up. Peasants burned farms, stole food, and attacked the wealthy British landlords. The British government, which ruled Ireland, declared a state of emergency and sent soldiers to the countryside to put down the rebellions. The British soldiers arrested any-

Mary Harris was born into a family of very poor farmers in southern Ireland.

one they suspected of fighting against the landlords. Many of the peasants hated anything and anyone who was British.

In this violent and unstable time, Mary Harris was born sometime between 1830 and 1844 in a village of County Cork, at the southern tip of Ireland. Her family had been poor peasants for generations. They rented their small cottage from a landlord. They ate what they could grow, which was mostly potatoes and oats.

As a very young girl, Mary saw violence and struggles for power all around her. Her grandfather and father joined the fight to free Ireland from Great Britain. Her grandfather, her father's father, was arrested by British soldiers and hanged for his part in the fight for Irish independence. Once a frightened Mary saw British soldiers marching through the streets of her village, carrying on their sharp bayonets the severed heads of rebel Irishmen.

Mary's father, Richard Harris, was afraid for his life. He knew that he had to escape the British soldiers or he, too, would be hanged for fighting against them. Leaving his wife and children behind, he fled from Ireland to the United States in about 1835. Mary's father was not alone in his decision to leave. In the 1840s and 1850s, about 1.5 million Irish people came to the United States. (Many of them came because of the failure of the potato crop upon which most of them had depended for food. Between 1846 and 1851, hundreds of thousands of poor Irish people starved to death in Ireland.)

Mary remembered how the British soldiers had come to her cottage soon after her father left. The soldiers yelled and demanded that he come out. When her mother told them that he was not home, they did not believe her, and they rushed into the cottage to look for him. They looked everywhere—they even tore down the chimney to see if he was inside. But they were too late. He was already gone.

Mary's father took a ship across the Atlantic Ocean to the United States. Along with thousands of other Irish immigrants, he took a low-paying job on a construction crew digging canals to link the waterways of New York State. Construction workers were paid 75 cents a day in the summer and 50 cents a day in the winter, when the days were shorter.

Richard Harris worked hard and carefully saved his money. Finally he had saved enough to pay for his family's passage from Ireland. Sometime around 1840 his wife and three children boarded a crowded immigrant ship that heaved and tossed its way across the ocean. The 3,000-mile trip from Ireland to New York took seven weeks, and the family was tired but happy when they joined him.

The Harrises settled in Toronto, Canada, where Mary's father

During the 1840s, thousands of people left Ireland for America.
Among them were Mary, her two brothers, and her mother.

took a job as foreman of a railroad-building crew. The Harris family had lived in Toronto for about two years when free public schools opened for the first time. Attendance was not required, so most children did not go. But Mary's father believed in the importance of a good education, and he sent all of his children to school.

There were not enough teachers in Mary's elementary school, so 75 or 100 children piled into each classroom. The older children helped the younger ones to study reading, writing, and arithmetic. Mary was a good student, and her parents were proud of her. At home in the evenings she learned the skill of dressmaking. Soon friends and neighbors were ordering dresses from her.

Mary's two brothers, Sean and Shamus, went to work on the railroad when they graduated from elementary school. But because she was such a good student, Mary's father insisted that she continue her education. She became the first person in the Harris family to graduate from high school.

Mary liked school so much that she decided to become a teacher. She studied for a year in a teachers' training school called a normal school. But when she was ready to teach, Mary could not get a job in Toronto, because she and her family were Roman Catholic, and the local schools did not hire Catholic teachers. So Mary left Canada. In 1859 she became an elementary school teacher at a Catholic school called St. Mary's in Monroe, Michigan. She taught there from August 1859 to March 1860, for a salary of $8 a month. That was a very low salary at a time when the average nonfarm worker earned about $30 a month. For some reason that historians have not been able to discover, Mary Harris never saw her family again after she left Canada. There is no further record of any letters or conversations between Mary and her family. Once she left Toronto, she was on her own.

CHAPTER TWO

A Young Woman Gains and Loses a Family

Schools in the late 1850s were very strict. Children had to memorize and recite long passages and obey their teachers without question. As a teacher, Mary Harris had to discipline her students if they did not obey her. After a year teaching school in Michigan, Harris grew tired of the strict discipline and decided that she did not want to be a teacher after all. Instead, she resolved to be a dressmaker. "I preferred sewing to bossing little children," she said later. She decided to go to Chicago and set up a dressmaking business.

But times were hard in Chicago. The economy was weak, and her dressmaking business did not do well. After a year, Harris realized that she was not making enough money to live. She needed to do something else. Reluctantly she decided to return to teaching, and she began to look for a teaching job.

Harris heard of the need for teachers in Memphis, Tennessee. She headed south and found that Memphis was very different from Chicago. The city had grown up beside the wide Mississippi River. Steamboats traveled up and down the river, carrying cotton and iron, which were then sent to other parts of the country on the new railroads. In Memphis, Harris got a job teaching elementary school during the 1860-61 school year. She was a pleasant young woman, about five feet tall, with bright blue eyes and wire-rimmed glasses. She usually wore a floor-length dress and generally had a bonnet on her head. On her feet she wore leather boots that laced up.

In 1861, she met George E. Jones, a tall, thin man with glasses. He had never been to school, but on his own he had learned to read and write. He and Mary Harris must have fallen in love quickly, for they got married two months after they met.

George was a skilled blacksmith and iron molder at a foundry called the Memphis Iron Works. His work as a molder was hot, tiring, and often dangerous. He melted iron in huge furnaces until it was a boiling liquid, which he poured into molds to make plows, stoves, horseshoes, and railroad tracks. George and the other iron molders worked 6 days a week, 12 hours a day, breathing the smoke, steam, and smell of molten iron. It was so hot in the foundry that their skin was scorched and their hair singed. In the summertime especially the heat in the foundry was almost unbearable.

George knew that industries—factories, mills, foundries, and mines—were just starting to grow in the United States. There were very few laws to protect the people who worked in industries. The owner of a factory, mine, or other business made all the decisions. Owners, who were called capitalists because they owned the capital or property, decided what to pay their workers and how long they should work. Most capitalists tried to make as much money as they could from their property. Usually this meant that they made their employees work as much as possible. Most working people spent 12 to 14 hours a day at their jobs, and for all that work they made very little money.

George Jones thought there should be a way to make his job better. He dreamed of having fresh air as he worked. He thought about working a shorter day, so he could spend more time with his new wife. He figured out ways that his boss could make iron molding a safer job.

But if George Jones asked his boss for changes alone, he would be fired. His boss had little interest in the health and happiness of his workers; he was only concerned with making money. Jones thought that the only way to make the foundry owner listen was for all the foundry workers to act together. Since the boss would not want to fire all his workers at once, they would have more of a chance of getting what they requested.

As early as the 1790s, different groups of workers in the United States had started to join together into organizations called unions, to protect themselves from their selfish employers and to gain more power to bargain with their bosses. George Jones met members of a union called the Iron Molders Union, which had formed in Philadelphia in the 1850s, and they explained to him how their union worked. The union encouraged all iron molders to get together and become members of a union at their foundry. Then the union members could ask their boss for higher wages or safer working conditions. Union representatives and the employer would sit down together and discuss worker demands. If the union members all asked together, their boss would be more likely to give them what they wanted. Such negotiation between union representatives and an employer is called collective bargaining. If the boss did not give them what they asked for, the union members might leave their job, or strike. The strike was the union's most powerful tool, for it was the threat of a strike that gave the union influence with an employer.

When the union members decided to strike, they set up human barriers called picket lines to prevent their boss from hiring new workers instead of agreeing to the union's demands. A picket line is a group of strikers who stand or march in a line in front of a mine or factory. Many strikers carry signs attached to long pieces of wood called pickets. These picketers demonstrate or protest against their employer's policies. By blocking the entrances, the strikers try to keep anyone from going in or out. Strikers call anyone who crosses a picket line and goes to work a strikebreaker or scab.

Mary Jones. No earlier photographs of her survive.

George Jones grew excited about the idea of employees working together in unions. He became a member of the Iron Molders Union. Soon he was visiting workers at other foundries, explaining to them the bargaining power of the union and encouraging them to join. Before they had children, Mary Jones often traveled with her husband. When she could not go with him, she listened to his stories and asked lots of questions whenever he returned home.

George and Mary Jones lived in a poor section of Memphis, not too far from the foundry where George worked. Their first child was born in January 1862. According to different accounts, Mary Harris Jones had between one and four children over the next four years. While the Joneses raised their children, the country was gripped by a terrible war.

In 1861, the issue of slavery had divided the United States into two societies. People in the Northern states wanted to end slavery. Slave owners in the Southern states wanted slaves to continue working on their farms. There seemed to be no room for compromise, and when people on both sides began to fight for the kind of society they wanted, the Civil War began. Tennessee was one of the 11 Southern states that seceded from the Union and joined the Confederate States of America. During the Civil War, the Southern city of Memphis was captured by Northern soldiers. Iron work was important in building war materials, and the Northern soldiers used the factories and foundries of Memphis to make guns and ammunition. George Jones, who had wanted to join the Northern army but was rejected for military service because of his poor eyesight, worked hard at the foundry and was paid well.

After the Northern victory and the Civil War's end in 1865, George Jones was hired as a full-time official of the Iron Molders Union. He traveled throughout Tennessee and nearby states, urging workers to join the union. By then the iron molders' national union was one of the country's strongest unions. At a time when employers insisted that people work at least 10 hours a day, the iron molders led the fight to shorten the workday to 8 hours. Six months after the end of the war, a local branch in Memphis was officially chartered by the Iron Molders Union.

In the 1860s, Memphis was an active, growing city, the sixth largest city in the South. The cotton and railroad industries brought many new people to the city. Memphis grew so quickly that public services could not keep up with the number of people. The drinking water was poor, there were no sewers, and garbage often piled up in the streets. The city was ripe for the spread of diseases.

The spring of 1867 in Memphis was very wet and rainy. When the rain finally ended, it left muddy streets, puddles, and ditches

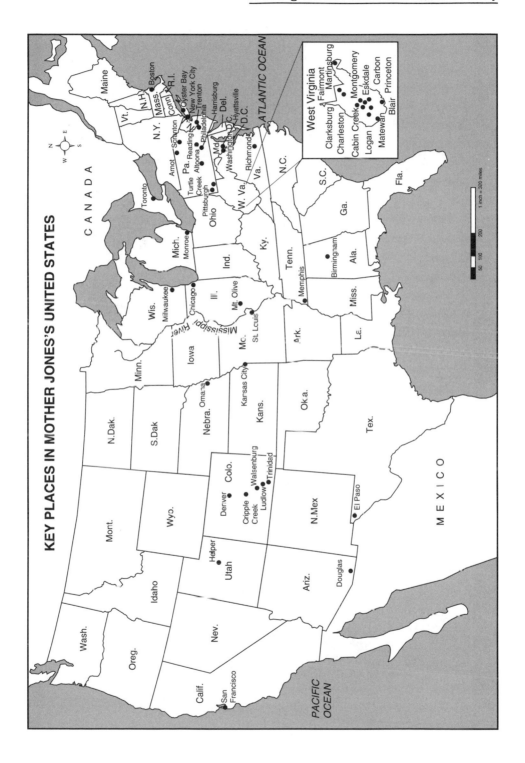

KEY PLACES IN MOTHER JONES'S UNITED STATES

West Virginia
Clarksburg
Fairmont
Martinsburg
Charleston
Cabin Creek
Montgomery
Eskdale
Logan
Carbon
Matewan
Blair
Princeton

full of standing water. Mosquitoes carrying the virus that causes a disease called yellow fever thrived in the still water. In the 1800s, yellow fever was one of the worst diseases in the world. People did not know that yellow fever came from a virus carried by mosquitoes, nor did they know that protecting drinking water and killing mosquitoes would prevent the disease.

The first things that happen to someone with yellow fever are chills, fever, headache, and back pains. In those days, without modern medicines, often their eyes, then their whole bodies, turned yellow. As the disease worsened, some victims turned black and their bodies began to smell horribly. As they neared death, they could not eat and their vomit was black. Unlike today, there was no known prevention or cure for yellow fever in 1867, and the disease was easy to catch. A yellow fever epidemic hit Memphis that summer, the first person dying of the disease in August.

Scenes of desperation were common during the 1867 yellow fever epidemic in Memphis.

People were very scared of yellow fever. The rich and those who had wagons or carriages quickly left the city to escape the disease. But poor people had no way to leave. Those still in Memphis burned sulfur and tar, thinking the smoke would protect them from the contagious fever. The burning tar let off a strong-smelling smoke that spread over the city and made the sky dull and hazy.

Public meetings were banned, and schools and churches were closed. People tried to stay in their houses as much as possible. They kept their windows and doors sealed shut. Doctors and nurses held rags or sponges over their noses as they went from house to house. Any house that held a yellow fever victim was quarantined—no one was allowed to go in or come out without official permission.

In all, 236 people died of yellow fever in Memphis that summer and fall. In the house across the street from George and Mary Jones, 10 people died from the fever. Finally in October the fever struck the Jones family. One by one, all of the Joneses' children died of yellow fever. The next week George Jones died. Mary Harris Jones was left all alone, childless and widowed. Later in her life, she wrote about this tragic time: "I sat alone through nights of grief. No one came to me. No one could. Other homes were as stricken as mine. All day long, all night long, I heard the grating of the wheels of the death cart [which went from house to house, picking up the bodies of those who had died]."

Soon after his death, George Jones's union held a special memorial meeting. The union honored him for the important work he had done on its behalf and it paid the funeral expenses for him and the children.

Mary Harris Jones felt terribly sad and empty without her family. To pass the time, she volunteered as a nurse, caring for others sick with the fever. There was little she could do for the dying, but she comforted their families. She took care of children whose parents were dying. She bathed the sick and cooked for those who could eat.

As winter approached and it grew colder in Memphis, the mosquitoes died, and the epidemic ended. Dejected and lonely, Mary Jones decided she needed to leave Memphis. Her husband's union collected some money for her, and she made plans to return to Chicago.

CHAPTER THREE

Disaster Leads to a New Life

Early in 1868, Mary Jones arrived in Chicago, where an old friend of hers suggested that she should open a dress shop again. She agreed, since she needed to make a living and she knew that work would help cure her sorrow at the loss of her family. She opened a small storefront shop with a room in the back where she slept at night.

Jones was surprised at how quickly the city of Chicago had grown during the Civil War. By the end of the war, there were almost 200,000 people living in the city. Some of them had become rich from selling grain and meat. But there were many poor people, too. The city was divided into rich and poor neighborhoods. The rich people had large, comfortable homes in the northeast, along Lake Michigan. Some even lived in huge mansions. The poor people lived on the south and west sides of the city, among the factories and slaughterhouses. Poor families were crowded into tiny wooden houses in neighborhoods that had no sewers or water pipes.

Jones's customers at the dress shop were rich Chicago women. Sometimes she went to their homes to fit their dresses or measure their curtains. In the wintertime, she could look out the windows of their fine, rich homes. She saw poor people who had no jobs or food. They shivered in the bitter wind as they walked along the frozen lake front. Jones began to see a big difference between the way these rich women lived and the lives of the poor people in Chicago.

Later in her life she would angrily call the rich women for whom she sewed "parlor parasites." A parasite is something that lives by taking nutrients from another creature, the way she believed rich people in Chicago lived at the expense of the poor. But for the time being she did not think of such things. She just worked. For almost four years she worked constantly. She had little time to make friends, and she did not get involved in the lives of her poor neighbors.

Then on Sunday, October 8, 1871, a great tragedy occurred. For months it had rained very little in Chicago. Wooden houses, warehouses, and factories, as well as Chicago's streets and sidewalks, which were also made of wood, were extremely dry. That night a fire started somewhere on the west side of the city. Burning the plentiful dry wood, the fire spread quickly. A strong wind blew the growing flames through downtown Chicago. As it burned for three days, the huge fire killed 250 people. It also destroyed hundreds of millions of dollars worth of property, leaving nearly four square miles of the city charred and flattened.

The fire turned Jones's business and her home to ash. For the second time in her life, all that Jones had was gone. She had no house, no clothes, no food, no family. The fire forced her to start her life over for the second time.

Mary Jones and 90,000 other people were left homeless. They

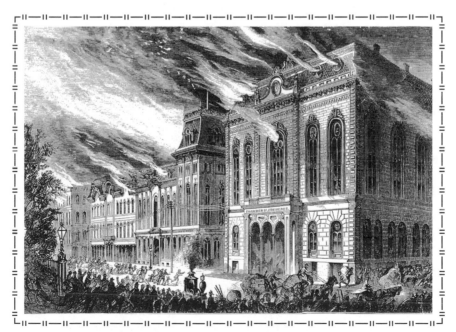

Mary Jones's dressmaking business was destroyed during the Great Chicago Fire of 1871.

spent the days after the fire camped out beside Lake Michigan, scrounging for scraps of food. Soon schools and churches opened for people to sleep in, and Jones found a place to stay in St. Mary's Church. Always an optimist, Jones sprang into action, helping to find rooms and food for the other homeless people. She kept busy, never letting her spirits sink or her energy fade. She met and comforted many working-class people who, like her, had lost everything they had in the fire.

Because of her late husband's work, she knew many of the iron molders in Chicago. They introduced her to members of the Knights of Labor, a union that had been started in 1869 by tailors in Philadelphia. The tailors encouraged all working people, no matter what their jobs, to join together in a single union. All across the country, many different kinds of workers became members of the Knights of Labor. They tried to get better working conditions and improve the lives of union members. The motto of the Knights was, "An injury to one is the concern of all."

Jones was very interested in the work of the Chicago Knights of Labor, whose members met every week in an old burned-out building. The Knights had to meet and work secretly, so that their bosses would not know of their plans. Employers did not like unions, because unions demanded better wages, shorter work days, and improved working conditions. Employers often fired union members and kept blacklists of all workers who the bosses thought were part of a union. Bosses shared their blacklists with each other, so if a worker was blacklisted, he would have a hard time finding another job in his trade or business.

Despite the threat to her work, Mary Jones found that she was spending less time at odd jobs as a dressmaker and more time speaking in public for the Knights of Labor. With her self-confidence and her loud clear teacher's voice, she was not afraid to stand up and address a group of people. By now her hair was white, and her blue eyes sparkled behind her wire glasses as she talked excitedly about the Knights. She spoke with energy and enthusiasm, and working people listened attentively. Soon she was visiting different parts of Chicago to tell workers about the Knights of Labor, always encouraging them to join the Knights.

Jones said whatever was on her mind. She did not worry

about being polite. She cursed industrialists, shocking some people with her use of four-letter words. She once explained why she cursed and swore. "I long ago quit praying and took to swearing. If I pray I will have to wait until I am dead to get anything, but when I swear I get things here." When Jones cursed, often it made people listen to find out why she was so angry.

Jones worked for the Knights through an economic depression that started in 1873. It was the worst economic depression that had hit the United States in all its history up to then. It lasted almost six years. During the depression, prices fell sharply and factories closed. Banks failed and thousands of businesses went bankrupt. Many thousands of workers lost their jobs or earned less money. Across the country, over 4 million people were without work. These people had no money to buy what they needed to survive. Thousands of homeless men and women ended up living in the streets and sleeping in public parks. Others traveled from town to town looking for work. In the cities, unemployed workers demanded jobs. Demonstrations and protests were often crushed by the police.

Jones noticed that, even during the depression, some people stayed rich. People who owned factories, mines, or other types of industry were called industrialists or capitalists. Most capitalists were able to hold on to their wealth and power during the depression. Jones grew to hate what she believed were the unfair differences in the living conditions of rich capitalists and poor workers. She thought the capitalists should share their wealth with their workers. After all, the workers were the ones who produced the goods that made capitalists rich. Jones devoted the rest of her life to helping workers get their fair share of the nation's wealth.

Members of the Knights of Labor told Jones about the theories behind a belief some of them held—socialism. According to them, socialism was a system in which workers would have their fair share of the wealth. Under socialism, no one rich person would own a factory or mine. Instead, the workers would own the factory themselves, and everyone would share the money made by the factory. Jones thought that socialism made sense.

Jones worked for the Knights of Labor, speaking at workers'

The work of 19th-century coal miners was difficult and dangerous.

meetings about the benefits of socialism. She argued and asked people questions. She used her gift of fiery speech to make workers laugh, cry, and get angry while they listened. Her speeches would make her famous—and infamous—later in her life.

By 1874, Jones worked full-time for the Knights, earning only a few dollars a week. She lived with union members' families and shared their food. When the Knights of Labor sent Jones to Pennsylvania that year, she helped with a strike by coal miners. At that time, coal was the biggest source of energy in the country. Trains and factories ran on coal, and coal was used to heat houses. So the coal miners' strike, which became known as the Long Strike since it lasted almost a year, was watched carefully all across the country.

In Pennsylvania, Jones saw for the first time the hard life led by coal miners. She saw the awful conditions under which they worked. Coal miners had one of the most dangerous jobs in the country. They worked deep underground in dark, narrow tunnels called mine shafts. They kneeled or stood in water all day, often bent over to reach the coal. Their heads and bodies were splashed with cold water dripping from above.

In the mines they breathed powder smoke (from the explosives they used to blast their way to the coal), gas, and coal dust. Many miners died from explosions and collapsing mine shafts. They could never predict when a mine shaft would collapse. A sudden collapse could trap a miner underground, crush his legs, or bury him alive.

Most miners were paid by the load of coal, not by the hour or day. Much of the work they did was called dead work. Drilling holes, repairing mine shafts, clearing away rocks, washing the coal, and building railroad tracks to haul the coal—all of these jobs were dead work, for which the miners were not paid. Even when the hardworking miners had mined a lot of coal, the mine owners' foremen would often say that the coal did not weigh as much as it really did. This short-weighting by the foremen meant that the coal miners ended up being paid less than they had fairly worked for.

Even outside the mines, the miners' lives were controlled by their bosses, the mining companies. Miners lived with their families in poorly built, drafty, company-owned houses. They bought their food and clothes from company-owned stores. If they were sick, they had to see a company doctor. Their children were taught in company schools.

Often the mining company printed its own money called scrip, which could not be spent like cash anywhere outside the company town. Miners paid in scrip could only spend it in company stores. The miners called the company stores "pluck-me stores" because they felt as if the companies could easily pluck whatever they wanted from the miners. The pluck-me stores charged higher prices than stores in other towns. A pair of shoes that cost $2.50 at another store might cost $4.00 at the pluck-me store. But since the miners had no cash, they could not go to other stores to buy things. If the miners got an increase in pay, then almost magically the prices in the company stores would go up. Often the miners were in debt to the mining company, for they had to spend more than they made just to buy the simplest food and clothing for their families.

If a miner complained, the company store refused to sell him anything, and he was forced out of his house. Miners could not hold meetings, have guests, or read books that were not approved by the company. In many mining towns, miners' wives and children also worked at difficult and exhausting jobs. Boys as young as six or seven years old worked in the breakers—windowless buildings just outside the mine entrance, where coal was separated from rocks and slate, broken into small pieces, and washed. Women and girls often worked in the small silk mills that grew up near mining towns.

The coal industry in Pennsylvania had grown tremendously

in the 1860s and early 1870s. Demands increased for iron plows and harvesters for farmers and iron rails, trains, and bridges for the railroads. The iron industry needed millions of tons of coal to fuel its growth. Dozens of small coal-mining businesses sprang up. They quickly came into conflict with their workers. Many of the Pennsylvania coal miners were Irish immigrants whose families had been poor peasants back in Ireland. Some of them had fought the British landlords in Ireland by using violence and by joining secret organizations such as one known as the Molly McGuires.

During the 1860s, over five dozen coal-mine foremen had been murdered. Many of these victims had been known for short-weighting. Mine owners and newspapers accused Irish immigrant workers of belonging to the Molly McGuires and of secretly planning the murders.

The situation had grown more tense during the Long Strike of 1874-75. The president of the big Reading Railroad had bought up many of the smaller coal-mining companies in eastern Pennsylvania. Then he had stored up an extra supply of coal and shut down the mines he owned in order to force the striking coal miners to give up. During the cold winter of 1874-75, the violence increased as the mine owners hired armed men who fired on protesting crowds. Union miners attacked strikebreakers with clubs and stones. The miners finally had to give up their strike and accept huge wage cuts.

Sometimes small children worked in the coal mines.

Soon after that, a series of murder trials known as the Molly McGuire trials were held. The coal-mine owners had hired special private police and detectives to participate at union meetings. These detectives claimed that the coal miners' union was really controlled by the Molly McGuires. At trials held in 1875 and 1876, 10 miners were found guilty of murder and sentenced to death by hanging. The trials did much to weaken public sympathy for the coal miners and their union.

Mary Jones had been shocked by the awful lives of the Pennsylvania coal miners. She had tried to comfort them and to encourage them to continue their Long Strike. Not long after the strike's failure and the Molly McGuire trials, Mother Jones heard disturbing news from another group of workers, the railroad workers.

Before the depression of the 1870s, the railroad industry made lots of money for its owners. The railroad owners were among the richest people in the country. But during the depression, railroad owners made less money, so they decided to cut their workers' wages. By 1876 workers' wages were one-third lower than they had been in 1873. The railroads also fired many workers and expected the smaller number of workers who were kept to do the same total amount of work as had been done before by the larger number of workers. Railroad workers ended up with longer working hours, often 15 or 18 hours a day.

In May 1877, representatives of four giant railroad companies met in Chicago and decided to cut their workers' pay by another 10 percent. On June 1, 1877, railroad workers on the Pennsylvania Railroad learned that they would be receiving the pay cut, the fourth since the depression started. On July 17, 1877, the news of a pay cut by the Baltimore and Ohio Railroad Company reached railroad workers in Maryland. Angry and exhausted, the railroad workers walked off the job. They refused to operate the trains unless the pay cut was canceled.

Encouraged by the action in Maryland, railroad workers in other states soon left their jobs. They acted as if they all belonged to one union. No one had planned such a huge strike, but the action by the railroad workers became the first national strike in U.S. history.

The railroad workers called on the Knights of Labor for advice. Mary Jones was sent to Pittsburgh, Pennsylvania, to help. She marched in picket lines with the strikers and collected food for the strikers' families, who had no income during the strike.

The strike, which became known as the Great Railway Strike of 1877, or the Great Uprising of 1877, spread to West Virginia.

27

Striking railroad workers stop a train in Martinsburg, West Virginia, in 1877.

There thousands of working families were angry at the railroads for not paying workers enough to live on. The governor of West Virginia sent the state militia, soldiers armed with guns, to guard railroad property in Martinsburg. There were fights between the soldiers and the strikers. When a state militia soldier shot and killed an unarmed striker, the striking railroad workers had had enough. Violence broke out, as angry crowds tore up rails and burned freight cars. A riot started and spread in all directions.

There were riots and strikes in other cities, too, from San Francisco to Chicago, from St. Louis to New York. In Chicago, for example, thousands of workers in many kinds of factories and shops joined the railroad strikers in a general strike. They marched through the streets gathering more and more support. The police fired into the crowds and battled strikers in the streets. In St. Louis, there was a mostly peaceful general strike. But that was not the case in Pittsburgh. There the Pennsylvania Railroad had decided to reduce the number of workers by using double-headers, extra-long trains pulled by two locomotives. That, combined with wage cuts, created great sympathy for the strikers.

On July 19, 1877, the mayor of Pittsburgh called out the local militia to keep order. The militia soldiers listened to the strikers' complaints and saw the unfair power held over them by the railroads. The soldiers agreed with what the strikers were saying, and they refused to fight the striking workers, joining them instead in their protest. Local shopkeepers and other working people, who understood the anger and the poverty of the railroad workers, also joined the crowd of strikers. The next day the strikers learned that the governor of Pennsylvania was sending militia from Philadelphia. The governor hoped that soldiers from farther away would not be so quick to agree with the strikers.

The Philadelphia militia came by train. Thousands of working people in Pittsburgh gathered on the train tracks to prevent the 600 soldiers from getting off the train. As the soldiers tried to make their way through the crowd, someone threw a rock at them. Immediately, the soldiers opened fire on the crowd. Twenty-six people, including some children, were killed by the soldiers' bullets.

The shootings made the crowd of more than 20,000 people even more desperate and angry, and they began to destroy Pennsylvania Railroad property. People rioted, burning and looting buildings, engines, passenger cars, and freight cars, and attacking the soldiers from Philadelphia.

The President of the United States, Rutherford B. Hayes, was very concerned about the local riots and strikes spreading throughout the United States. Fearing the situation would soon get out of control, he called out federal soldiers to stop the violence. Using more violence, the federal soldiers drove the crowds away and broke the strike. U.S. troops were used in Pittsburgh, Indianapolis, East St. Louis, Chicago, and elsewhere. In all, at least 100 people were killed during the strikes, most of them shot by state government soldiers. Three hundred others were wounded. By August 2, the Great Uprising was over, and many railroad workers found themselves fired from their jobs for taking part.

The violent national strike had frightened state governments and capitalists into violent response. Workers started to believe that the state and federal governments did whatever the wealthy capitalists said. Workers and the members of the community who had joined them were shocked to discover that state and federal officials would use the force of state militias and the U.S. Army against them. They were, after all, American citizens, and their strike had been the only way they had to stop the railroads from cutting their wages again.

But despite their surprise at the government's reaction, workers were hopeful about making their lives better. The workers had seen for the first time how powerful they could be if they were united in a union.

CHAPTER FOUR

Jones Learns More About Unions and Workers

Industrialists did little to improve workers' wages and hours or to recognize their unions in the 1880s. The decade, therefore, was full of strikes. In one year there were nearly 1,600 strikes across the country involving about 610,000 workers. Many workers joined unions, hoping that by joining together, they would have more bargaining power with the industrialists who ignored them as individuals. The Knights of Labor had 702,000 members at its peak in 1886.

Mary Jones traveled frequently in the 1880s, speaking for the Knights of Labor. But she spent most of her time in Chicago, where she still worked odd jobs as a dressmaker. She saw a divided city: many poor, unhappy, and hungry people, living in the same city with some very rich people. The industrialists, who owned factories, mills, and mines, made lots of money. One of the reasons they were able to make so much money was that they made workers spend long days at their jobs producing goods. Often factory, mill, and mine workers labored for 10, 12, or even 14 hours every day.

Workers who joined unions at this time wanted to change many things about their jobs. But one thing was clearly most important to them: Workers wanted to shorten the long days that they were made to work. Mary Jones knew that workers were unhappy about their long workdays. She had heard their complaints at many union meetings.

Searching for ways to help the workers, Jones went to meetings of new radical groups and political parties. These new groups were set up by people who were frustrated by the control that powerful industrialists had over the economy. These people thought the system of labor was fundamentally unfair. Why should the owner who did no labor himself get the profits of industry? Why should working people have no control over their work? Why should their children die young because their parents could not afford to pay a doctor? Why should some people live without heat, running water, or toilets while their bosses owned luxurious mansions?

Some of the people asking these questions were called anarchists. Anarchists believed that the government was controlled by rich industrialists and that it would be better not to have a government at all. Anarchists believed that without a government people could make their own decisions about their lives. They could build communities that respected the equal rights of all members. They could work reasonable hours and share the products of their labor. No one would be controlled by industrialists.

In Chicago a small group of anarchists joined forces with unions and workers' groups who said they should have to work only eight hours a day. With eight-hour workdays, they would have eight hours to sleep and eight hours a day when they could be with their families, read, work for the community, attend meetings, and enjoy life. Huge crowds came to the shore of Lake Michigan, where the anarchists and other workers held meetings about the eight-hour workday.

The anarchists had a plan for the "Eight Hour Movement." They asked workers nationwide to join in the demand for an eight-hour workday by participating in a national strike in all trades—a general strike—on May 1, 1886. If no one worked, the industrialists could not make money. The striking workers would agree to come back to work, but only for eight hours a day. If the industrialists wanted to make money, they would have to give the workers an eight-hour workday.

Mary Jones did not believe in anarchism, but she was active in the "Eight Hour Movement." She was in Chicago for the demonstration on May 1. Thousands of workers in Chicago supported the national strike. In some other areas of the country, employers did grant an eight-hour workday to their workers as a result of the strike, but bosses in Chicago made no concessions. Workers there were angry that their employers ignored their demands.

Even after the national strike ended, workers on the south side of Chicago kept up their long strike at the McCormick har-

31

vester plant, which produced farming equipment. Scabs had been working in the factory since February. At that time the company had locked out the regular workers over a dispute about unionization. Two days after the May 1 national strike, the striking workers held a meeting outside the factory. Inside the factory, strikebreaking scabs continued to work. Strikers hated scabs, because they weakened the strike. As long as enough scabs worked, the bosses did not have to give the strikers what they wanted.

When the scabs at the McCormick harvester plant finished their shift, they came outside to return home. The scabs and the strikers started to argue, and a huge fight started. Someone called the police. When the police arrived, they fired their guns into the fight. Their bullets killed four people and wounded several others. Other people were trampled under the hooves of the police horses.

This violence between working people and police made the anarchists very angry. The anarchists blamed the police for the violence. Because the police were part of the government, the anarchists said again that there should be no government. The anarchists called on workers to come to a meeting to hear more about their point of view.

The meeting was held on the evening of May 4, 1886, in a part of Chicago called Haymarket Square. Mary Jones was among the 3,000 people who gathered in the square to hear anarchists and other labor speakers talk about what workers should do. The meeting was quiet and peaceful. Police stood at the edge of the crowd of people. The anarchists told their points of view, protesting police brutality and calling for workers to unite. Other labor leaders spoke. Jones left with many others around 9:30 P.M. when it began to rain.

Around 10:00 P.M., during the last speech, the police started to break up the meeting. Then someone threw a dynamite bomb into the small crowd. It exploded among the group of police, killing several policemen. Surprised by the sudden blast, the remaining police fired their guns through the darkness on the several hundred people who had been listening to the speeches. People in the crowd who had guns shot back at the police. The dark night was filled with the sounds of screams, gunshots, and the thuds of falling bodies. Desperately people tried to run away from the awful violence. When the shooting was over, 7 policemen and 10 workers were dead. More than 200 people were wounded.

The bombing and subsequent shootings in Haymarket Square scared the leaders of the city of Chicago, who quickly declared a state of emergency. They banned public meetings and arrested hundreds of people in working-class neighborhoods. Public leaders and the press blamed unions for the Haymarket violence. The public began to think that anything the unions did was violent. The reputation of unions was severely tarnished, and the "Eight Hour Movement" ended.

Even today no one knows who threw the bomb, but newspapers and public opinion held that the anarchists were responsible. Enemies of the labor movement pointed accusing fingers at anyone associated with unions. Several anarchist labor leaders were blamed for throwing the bomb. Eight men were arrested and put in jail. At their trial, the anarchists were found guilty of murder. Outside the courthouse, a crowd of about 1,000 people cheered the verdict. Seven of the prisoners were sentenced to die and one to 15 years in prison.

Mary Jones had left the crowd before violence broke out at Chicago's Haymarket Square on May 4, 1886.

Over the next year, as the verdict was appealed, public opinion changed. People across the United States and Europe urged that the anarchists' lives should be spared. The governor received petitions signed by 200,000 people. Just before the hanging, one of the condemned men committed suicide in his cell. A few hours later, the sentences of two of the men were changed to life in prison. In November 1887 the four remaining men were hanged in front of 200 witnesses. After the hangings, the funeral procession stretched for many blocks, as thousands of sad workers followed the black hearses that carried the bodies of the hanged men. Thousands more, dressed all in black, lined the streets for miles. (Seven years later a new governor of Illinois was elected. He read through the papers from the anarchists' trial and decided that they had all been innocent. Realizing that public fear and panic had led to improper convictions, he gave full pardons to the three men who were still in jail.)

During the 1886 trial, leaders of the Knights of Labor had been afraid to try to help the condemned anarchists, because they did not want to be associated with the Haymarket bombing. Many workers were disappointed that the Knights did not try to help. The Haymarket bombing, combined with the failure of an important railroad strike in the Southwest and the failure of the May 1886 general strike, weakened the Knights of Labor. More than 200,000 members, including Mary Harris Jones, soon left the Knights.

Even though she was no longer part of the union, Mary Jones continued to travel on her own, going wherever workers were trying to make their lives better. She took a train to a coal miners' strike in Norton, Virginia, in 1891. At the train station, she learned from a coal miner about the local coal company's dishonest practices. He showed her the railroad tracks and the freight cars filled with coal. The miner told Jones that he and the other miners had made a contract with the coal company to fill those cars for a certain amount of pay. After they signed the contract, the company put lower bottoms in the cars. Now each car held a ton more coal than when the contract had been made.

Jones understood the power of the mining companies and the unfairness with which they treated their workers. During her lifetime she would struggle many times with coal companies, from Pennsylvania to West Virginia to Colorado. This time, however, even her feisty determination was not enough to help the miners, and the strike was lost. The coal miners could not survive and support their families without the small wages they earned from mining. Dejectedly they went back to work with the same unfair weighing system that they had struck against.

Between 1893 and 1898, the United States experienced another terrible depression. It was even worse than that of the 1870s. In 1893, the Philadelphia and Reading Railroad company failed, and the stock market crashed. Hundreds of banks and thousands of companies went bankrupt. By 1894, many other major railroad and steel companies also went out of business. About one of every five workers was unemployed. Thousands of homeless people traveled the country's roads looking for work in other towns.

Many people demanded that the federal government provide some sort of relief and jobs. Jacob S. Coxey, an Ohio businessman, called for the unemployed to march to Washington, D.C., to

During 1894, many out-of-work people in what was called
Coxey's Army marched to Washington, D.C., to demand jobs.

protest unemployment. He wanted a huge demonstration there in favor of new laws. These laws would provide money to communities to pay the unemployed people to work on public improvements such as roads.

In 1894, more than a dozen different groups—calling themselves Coxey's Army—began traveling eastward from the West and Midwest. Sympathetic farmers and workers gave them food along the way. Sometimes the marchers seized trains for transportation, but U.S. troops soon put a stop to that. Mary Jones helped feed a column of these marchers when they passed through Chicago. Of the 20,000 people in the groups, only about 600 reached Washington, D.C. Coxey was arrested and jailed and the makeshift army disbanded.

In 1894, railroad workers across the country went on a strike that came to be called the Pullman strike. George M. Pullman, a powerful industrialist, had built the company town of Pullman near Chicago. There factory workers lived and built Pullman sleeping cars for railroad use. When the depression began in 1893, he had laid off thousands of workers and had cut wages by 25 percent. But he had refused to lower the rents and other charges in his company town. When Pullman fired some workers who complained about this, the strike began in May.

Soon the new American Railway Union, led by Eugene V. Debs, decided to boycott, that is, refuse to work on, any train that used Pullman cars. When workers in one place or industry refuse to work in order to support and show solidarity with striking workers in another place or industry the strike is called a sympathy strike. The sympathy strike in support of the Pullman workers shut down railroads across the country.

Much of the violence in the Pullman strike occurred in the Chicago area. But the governor of Illinois refused to call out the state militia because he sympathized with the strikers. The railroad companies, however, had a plan to crush the strike. They got the federal government to attach mail cars to trains that also had Pullman cars. Officials then said that strikers were interfering with the U.S. mails. A federal court issued an injunction—a court order—that strikers must not interfere with the mail service. President Grover Cleveland then ordered 2,500 federal troops to

The Pullman Strike of 1894 ended after President Grover Cleveland sent U.S. troops into the Chicago area.

Chicago to enforce the court order. Within a week the strike was crushed.

During the Pullman strike, Mary Jones had traveled to Birmingham, Alabama, where 8,000 coal miners were also striking. After the Pullman strike was crushed, Eugene V. Debs, leader of the American Railway Union, came to address the striking miners to show his support for their strike. Mary Jones helped organize a crowd that met Debs at the Birmingham train station. By that time, Debs was becoming one of the nation's most famous labor leaders, and Mary Jones would work with him again in years to come.

Meanwhile, in Birmingham, the scab coal miners kept working and the state militia guarded trains loaded with coal, so the mines stayed open. The miners held out for five months, but in the end the strike was broken. Miners could no longer survive without their wages, so they had to go back to work.

After the miners' strike was broken in Alabama, Mary Jones

wanted to see how children were treated in the Southern cotton mills. She had seen the bleak conditions facing adult labor in the South, but recently she had heard even more terrible stories about child labor. The growth of factories between 1870 and 1900 led to a million more children working in textile (cloth) mills. Children as young as six or seven went to work all day just like adults. Many worked 10-hour days for 30 cents a day. In 1900, about 30 percent of the mill workers in the South were under the age of 16. Factory and mill owners liked to hire child workers because they worked for less money and didn't talk back or go out on strike.

The children of rich and middle-class parents went to school. Children like Mary Harris went to school because their parents knew an education was important. But many poor children did not have time to play or go to school. They went to work because their families needed the money. If their children did not work, these poor families would not have enough to eat. Parents sent their children to work, even though according to some local and state laws their children were too young to work legally.

Mary Jones saw children like this working in cotton mills.

Mary Jones knew these things when she took some time off from her work helping the miners' union to get a job in a cotton mill in Alabama in 1894. The owner of the cotton mill only hired Jones when she said she had six children that she would bring from the North to work. As Jones worked in the mill, she saw little children work all day. Whole families got up at 4:30 in the morning, when the overseer's whistle blew. Even the six- and seven-year-olds were at work in the mill by 5:30 A.M. They worked for 14 hours every day.

The child workers fell asleep over their lunches, and their faces were splashed with cold water to wake them up again. After work, these children walked home, ate supper, and soon fell asleep again. They had no time for play or school. Work was their whole life.

When the mill owner began to get suspicious that Jones had no children of her own to work for him, she quit her job. She moved on, visiting and working in other Southern towns. In Selma, Alabama, Jones rented a room from a mother and her 11-year-old daughter Maggie, both of whom worked in the local mill. One day Maggie got her hair caught in the fast-moving mill machinery. Her scalp was torn off by the strong machine, and she died. While other workers carried the dead girl's body back from the mill to the family's small house, Mary Harris Jones watched with a mixture of sadness and fury.

Mary Jones was angered by the dreadful lives of the children she saw in the South. She went to New York to tell people about the terrible conditions the children suffered. For a long time after she left the South, Jones had trouble eating. She felt as if all the food she ate and the clothes she wore were produced by the hard work of sad children. "I declare," Mary Jones said, "that their little lives are woven into the cotton goods they weave; that in the thread with which we sew our babies' clothes, the pure white confirmation dresses of our girls, our wedding gowns and dancing frocks, in that thread are twisted the tears and heartache of little children."

Jones thought that part of the adult and child workers' problem was the newspapers of the day, which usually sided with the capitalists. They generally printed only the business owners' and bosses' point of view. Jones thought the workers needed their own paper. Her idea was for a paper that would educate workers, allow them to express their own opinions, and explain how socialism could help them. She believed that a socialist system would be better for workers, allowing them to own factories, work cooperatively, and share equally in the wealth they pro-

39

duced. In the 1890s, Jones helped to set up a socialist workers' weekly newspaper called *Appeal to Reason* in Kansas City.

Appeal to Reason started publication in August 1895 during the continuing depression. It spoke out against rich, powerful industrialists and listed books explaining socialism for workers to read. Its articles described socialism as a reasonable alternative to the unfair capitalist system of labor. With conviction and enthusiasm, Jones traveled and sold subscriptions for the new paper to people, including coal miners in Pennsylvania and soldiers at the army barracks in Omaha, Nebraska. In time, *Appeal to Reason* had half a million subscribers.

As Mary Jones traveled for *Appeal to Reason*, she discussed socialism with the people she met. She got involved in political parties that worked to get socialists into the government. In 1895, she joined the Socialist Labor party in Kansas City. She attended a meeting of a number of socialists on June 15, 1897, when Eugene V. Debs organized a group called the Social Democracy of America.

Socialists had many disagreements among themselves about the best way to change society. Some encouraged violence and destruction of property; others wanted to make changes peacefully. In 1901, many smaller socialist groups put aside their differences and united to form the Socialist Party of America. Jones became part of that group. (She would later be expelled from the Socialist party, after she wrongly claimed that the party's secretary was dishonest.)

Jones kept thinking and speaking about socialism and what it meant for workers. By 1904, there were 4,000 strikes a year across the country. Hundreds of thousands of people were thinking and dreaming of living in a socialist society, and some of these people were beginning to act on their dreams by striking. They believed that there was enough wealth in the United States for everyone to live comfortably, if only that wealth were not hoarded by rich capitalists. Socialists wanted to redistribute the wealth of the capitalists, sharing it among everyone. This idea made the capitalists very nervous, for they did not want to give up their wealth or power, and they began to search for ways of preventing socialism from happening.

CHAPTER FIVE

A White-Haired Woman Becomes "Mother" to the Miners

Many small coal and metal miners' unions had been part of the Knights of Labor. When the Knights lost much of its membership and power in the late 1880s, a number of small miners' unions left them and formed the United Mine Workers of America, or UMW. During the 1890s, Mary Harris Jones began to work as a volunteer for the United Mine Workers. The miners who made up the UMW, most of whom were coal miners, would become some of Jones's most devoted followers.

Mary Harris Jones was about 60 years old. She looked like somebody's grandmother with her white hair and wearing a long dark dress with a lace collar and long sleeves. Like most women

A union poster. During the 1890s, Mary Jones began to help organize local groups of the United Mine Workers of America.

of her day, Mary Jones usually wore a large hat with a wide brim.

But Jones's strong beliefs and her struggle against unfair practices made her different from most other women of her day. Few other women would talk back to police and rich company owners. Few other women would visit miners in the deep, dark mine shafts. Jones was glad to be different, for she had little patience with the women of her day, whom she called "poor, ignorant geese" because they flocked to do and wear the same thing. "It nauseates me to see your average city woman," said Jones. "She is always overdressed, and although she wears gloves she is careful to leave her right hand bared so that she can display her fingers crowded to their utmost with jewels. Whenever I see that sort of display, I think of the gems as representing the blood of some crucified child."

Mary Harris Jones knew a very different way of life, the horrible life of the coal miners and their families. In the mining towns, she saw deep poverty and unhappiness. Babies were hungry, and children were barefoot. Miners' families lived in drafty, bare shacks.

Jones wanted to help miners. While she had worked with unions for several years, now she decided to become a full-time union organizer. An organizer is a person who tells all the workers in one mine or factory about the union and encourages them to join. If all its workers join the union, a mine or factory is called organized, and the union can then make demands that the boss change things.

In Jones's lifetime, union organizers led dangerous lives. The bosses and industrialists did not like unions or their organizers because they realized that unions took power away from them. Unions gave workers the power to make collective decisions about their work. To prevent unions from organizing in their businesses, employers began to hire spies who gave the bosses reports on the activities of their workers. Sometimes workers joined the union outside the workplace and then would try to organize workers at the place of business. If a worker was found to be a union member, the boss fired him.

In 1897, Jones went to the dangerous West Virginia mining districts, where mining companies were working hard to prevent unions from entering the region. The companies knew that organized miners would weaken their powerful hold on the area, so they threatened miners who joined the union. Many union miners were arrested, fired, and blacklisted. Bosses fired miners who were seen talking with Jones and the other organizers.

The mining companies hired armed company guards to patrol the area around their mines. These guards often beat and arrested strikers and organizers. The local police and judges usually did nothing to protect the rights of strikers or union organizers. Either the police and the judges were scared by the mining companies or they agreed with them that unions were bad.

Because of the spies, the blacklists, and the guards, the UMW in West Virginia had to work secretly. Union organizers held meetings after dark in the woods. Often after the meetings, Jones would walk home several miles through rain and mud. She found her way home by following railroad tracks in the dark.

During the 1890s, the average life expectancy for a woman in the United States was not quite 50 years. Mary Harris Jones was already in her sixties, but she worried little about her own health or safety. She would sleep anywhere she could lie down and eat any kind of food that she was offered. She gave away whatever clothes she could spare to the poor people she met. Jones brought new energy and hope to the striking miners. Even though she was the age of many of their grandmothers, she hiked around in the mountains and was not scared by the guards or the bosses. If she could do these things the miners began to believe that they could, too.

In the dangerous work of union organizing, it sometimes helped that Jones was a woman. Often soldiers or police treated her better than they treated the male miners. They did not want to beat or harm a woman. Jones learned this and took advantage of it for the rest of her life, going where men could not go and saying what men could not say.

She convinced many West Virginia miners to join the United Mine Workers. But even with the hard work of Mary Jones and the other union organizers, the mining companies were too powerful. A strike against wage cuts, part of a nationwide strike, began in early July 1897 but did not seem to affect the compa-

43

nies, who had hired armed guards and strikebreaking scabs to continue the work in the mines. After 12 weeks the strike was called off. The UMW organizers left West Virginia, but Mary Harris Jones knew that someday they would be back.

Next, Jones went to the Pennsylvania mining region, where the United Mine Workers was trying to organize the miners into local unions. Jones worked in areas where many of the miners and their families were Irish immigrants. The immigrants felt close to her because she came from Ireland, too. When she spoke at a meeting, Jones's voice was deep and powerful. When she became excited about her subject, her voice dropped even lower. Miners claimed to feel Mary Jones's strong words race through their bodies.

Soon Jones became famous. When people found out that she was going to speak at a meeting, they gathered in large crowds. Sometimes thousands of excited workers, men and women, young and old, came to hear her speak. Jones called the miners "her boys."

When she spoke, Jones was not a "lady." She used the language of the miners, which was often rough. She would take a drink of beer with "her boys," something most women would not have done. Because she was like them, the miners and their families loved Mary Harris Jones. She was a sign of hope that their lives could be better. She took care of them, and she loved them. Some miners and their families called Jones "the Angel of the Miners." Others thought Jones was like a mother to them, and they began to call her "Mother Jones." Soon the nickname stuck. She was known to workers as Mother Jones for the rest of her life.

For much of the time from 1897 to 1900, Mother Jones worked on United Mine Workers' strikes in Pennsylvania. Coal miners were striking for union recognition, a shorter workday, an increase in their pay, and a decrease in prices of mining supplies like gunpowder, which the miners had to buy themselves. The miners also wanted to be paid in cash, so they would not have to buy from the company stores.

The mining companies did not give in to the strikers' demands. After a while, the miners began to lose faith in the effectiveness of striking. They had no income while they were on strike, and they worried about how their families would live. The miners began to think that strikes would not work. Mother Jones went from mining camp to mining camp, encouraging the striking coal miners to keep up the fight.

She spoke to 10,000 strikers and sympathizers in Turtle Creek, near Pittsburgh. She encouraged them to fight for their rights. She asked farmers in the area to share their food with the strikers, and she organized strikers' wives into picket lines. She led the strikers' children in parades in support of their parents. One little girl carried a homemade banner that read, "Our Papas Aren't Scared." All of the activity that Mother Jones created convinced the Turtle Creek miners to continue their strike.

Mother Jones visited a town called Plumb Creek. There the striking miners were living in tents because the coal company had thrown them out of their company-owned houses. The coal company was trying to force the miners back to work by sending deputy sheriffs to drag the men into the mines.

One 13-year-old girl watched as the sheriffs came to take her father from their tent. The girl ran into the tent and came back out with a shotgun. It was so heavy she could only hold one end off the ground, but she pointed it at the sheriffs and said, "Now you just let go of my papa, and if you don't this gun will shoot every one of you bad men." The sheriffs were not sure what she would do. They were afraid she might shoot them, so they released her father. The little girl became a hero to the miners. Her courage raised their spirits and helped them to continue the strike. Mother Jones was proud of the girl.

In the spring of 1899, Mother Jones went to a mine called Drip Mouth in Arnot, Pennsylvania. There striking Irish immigrants had been replaced by scabs, and armed company guards prevented the strikers from interfering in the scabs' work. The striking miners were hungry and discouraged. Some called for an end to the strike. Mother Jones responded quickly and angrily. "Quitters! A fine bunch you are! A disgrace to Ireland! If you can't win the strike, I'll get your wives, daughters and sisters to fight your battles!"

She did what she said. The next morning she told the men to stay home with the children. Then she gathered all the women

Breaker boys were children who broke up and cleaned large chunks of coal. They worked for very little money.

and told them to bring brooms, mops, frying pans, and rolling pins. Mother Jones thought it would be better if she herself did not lead the women as they marched. As their leader, she chose a big woman with a little red shawl tied over her wild red hair. The woman's face was red, and her eyes were mad. The woman wore one black stocking and one white stocking and a red petticoat.

Led by this woman, the miners' wives and daughters marched confidently off to the mine entrance, afraid of nothing. At the entrance to the mine, they found the scabs getting ready to lead their mules into the shaft. Shouting and banging their pans, the women scared the scabs' mules. The frightened mules bucked and kicked and ran off. The fearless women then chased the guards and the scabs away from the mine and set up picket lines around the entrance.

For days and nights the women guarded the entrance to the mine. They stood watch with a broom or mop in one hand and some with a baby in the other. No scabs could enter the mine, and no coal could be brought out of the mine. The strike was back on track, and the miners thanked their wives and Mother Jones.

Several more times during the strike, Mother Jones would organize the women to march with their brooms and pans. Then one day the new president of the United Mine Workers, John Mitchell, asked her to stop organizing the women's marches. Mitchell had been told by local police that they would use force to stop the marches, and he did not want to have any violence during the strike.

But these victories by the marching women, when they closed mines to scabs, had given the miners new hope. They stayed with the strike. The local mine company eventually gave in at the end of February 1900, granting the miners a 10 percent wage increase. The people of Arnot knew Mother Jones had played a major role in winning the strike, and they gave her a good-bye party in the local opera house.

Since 1897, Mother Jones and the UMW had been working hard to organize Pennsylvania mines. The success of the small, local strike in Arnot was a sign to UMW leaders that the union was strong enough in Pennsylvania to call a larger strike. On September 17, 1900, the UMW did just that, and one week later, 127,000 miners—union and non-union—were refusing to work. This larger strike was so effective that mine owners agreed to settle it on October 29, giving pay increases but no recognition of the union.

While future strikes would not be so peaceful, the miners' strikes in Pennsylvania ended with very little violence and no riots or bloodshed. By winning the strikes and gaining an eight-hour workday for miners in the region, the UMW became quite popular. It raised its national membership to 115,000.

Everyone talked about Mother Jones's hard work in these strikes. They said that she had done the best organizing work for the UMW. They said that she could talk anyone into joining the union. They said that it was because of her that the miners stuck together and the strikes were won.

Shortly after the settlement of the Pennsylvania strikes, the UMW and Mary Harris Jones returned to West Virginia to try again to establish the union there. When she spoke to the miners' meetings, Mother Jones would shout, stomp her feet, and gesture with her hands. Another union organizer who was in the area said, "Our meetings were very tame indeed, until we were blessed with the presence of a new force. This new force is just what is needed. Mother Jones is attracting great attention and her meetings every night are increasing the enthusiasm for the union."

Often Jones would yell at the miners. She told them they were worth nothing if they did not join the union. She scolded them as if she really were their mother, but everyone knew she loved "her boys," the miners. After she spoke, she greeted them with a firm, friendly handshake.

In one West Virginia town, the union organizers paid a priest so they could hold their meetings in the local church. Mother Jones found out and angrily took back the money from the priest. She told the union members to meet in the town's schoolhouse instead. "Your organization is not a praying institution," she told them. "It's a fighting institution. . . . Pray for the dead and fight like hell for the living!"

A West Virginia town called Kelly Creek was especially well guarded by the mining companies. Even the UMW had given up on trying to reach the town's miners with news of the union. But Mother Jones refused to give up. She sneaked close to the town and held a secret night meeting in the woods, where she helped miners join the union. The next day 40 of the new union members were fired. There had been spies at the night meeting who reported the names of the miners to the coal company. But despite fear for their jobs, miners knew what they could gain if they worked together, and they continued to join the union.

Mother Jones was a brave and stubborn woman who would not let concern for her own safety interfere with her union organizing. When she went to speak to a group of miners in Mt. Carbon, West Virginia, home of the Tianawha Coal and Coke Company, an official of the company told the local sheriff, "Tell that woman she cannot speak here tonight; if she tries, I will jail her." The sheriff told Mother Jones what the company official said. She answered that she was not looking for trouble, but if trouble came, she would not run away from it. "I am going to speak here tonight," she said. "When I violate [break] the law, and not until then will you have any right to interfere." The official and the sheriff went off to look up the law. Mother Jones saw no more of them.

One night after a union meeting she and three miners were going to catch the train to return to town. She rode in a small horse-drawn buggy; the miners walked behind. She arrived first at the spot where they were to meet the train together and waited by the train tracks. When Mother Jones realized the train was about to come and the three miners still had not appeared, she grew worried.

Suddenly she heard shouts of "Murder! Murder!" Two of the miners appeared. Breathlessly they told Mother Jones that armed guards had attacked them in the dark. They had escaped, but the guards were still beating the third miner, whose name was Jo. Just then Mother Jones heard the train coming. She had an idea.

"Jo! Jo! The boys are coming," she yelled as loudly as she could. "They're coming! The whole bunch's coming. The car's almost here!" The armed guards, who thought that a huge group of miners was coming on the approaching train, ran off. The guards left poor Jo lying on a bridge, blood streaming from cuts on his head. Mother Jones responded quickly. She tore her petticoat in strips and bandaged his head. Then she and the other miners helped him onto the train, which was empty. There was no huge group of miners coming. Mother Jones had bluffed their way out of a dangerous situation.

This attack on Jo was only one example of the increasing violence against union miners. Many times gunmen hired by the local mining companies sneaked into the miners' houses at night, shooting and killing sleeping miners who they thought had union connections. Sometimes they shot the miners' wives and children, too. The increasing violence made Mother Jones even angrier with the bosses and industrialists who owned the mining companies. Mother Jones knew that they hired guards who beat and arrested miners. She knew that they were getting rich while the miners lived poorly.

On January 25, 1901, Mother Jones spoke for the first time at the annual convention of the United Mine Workers of America. She spoke out against the bosses and industrialists:

> They have built their mines and breakers to take your
> boys out of the cradle; they have built their factories
> to take your girls; they have built on the bleeding,
> quivering hearts of yourselves and your children
> their palaces. They have built their magnificent
> yachts and palaces; they have brought the sea from
> mid-ocean up to their homes where they can take
> their baths—and they don't give you a chance to go
> to the muddy Missouri and take a bath in it.

Mother Jones was right about the way miners were treated. One well-publicized case was that of a 12-year-old boy named Andy Chippie. Andy worked in the coal mines of West Virginia. He worked all day in the mines and made 40 cents a day. His father had been killed in a mining accident four years earlier. Andy had to give all of his earnings back to the coal company to pay off debts left by his father. Andy and his family grew poorer and poorer.

Mother Jones hated the inequality between families like Andy's and rich mining company owners. Mother Jones grew angrier and angrier at the mining companies, and her anger made her more and more brave. She was not afraid of armed mine guards or local police. She was arrested for the first of many times in 1902. At the time, she was organizing for the United Mine Workers in the Fairmont coal field in northern West Virginia. There the Consolidated Coal Company had managed to keep the union out for the past ten years.

First Tom Haggerty, the head UMW organizer, was arrested. Mother Jones carried on the union organizing after he was arrested. On June 20, while she was speaking at a rally near a mine in Clarksburg, a federal marshal began arresting other organizers in the crowd that had gathered to hear her. Mother Jones realized as she spoke that she was going to be arrested as well. She kept on talking until she had finished her speech. The last thing she said to the crowd was: "Goodbye, boys; I'm under arrest. I may have to go to jail. I may not see you for a long time. Keep up this fight! Don't surrender!"

As she stepped down from the speaking platform, she was

arrested for violating a court injunction. An injunction is an order from a judge against a particular action. This injunction was against union organizers holding a meeting within sight of the coal company property. The marshal who arrested Mother Jones tried to give her special treatment because she was a woman. He offered to let her stay in a hotel room instead of a jail cell until her trial. Proudly she refused special treatment, choosing instead to go to the jail house with the others who had been arrested.

At her trial, Mother Jones was firm as she faced federal judge John J. Jackson. Judge Jackson told Mother Jones not to violate his injunction. She responded that she would not violate the law. She would continue doing the work she had been doing. If that violated his injunction, she said, she feared that it would be violated. Disrespectfully she called him a scab. The judge told her she should get involved in a charity organization. She told him that she wanted justice, not charity. Her words attracted national newspaper attention.

Judge Jackson sentenced the other union organizers to jail terms, but he dismissed Mother Jones with a scolding. He thought that if he sent her to jail, she would use the publicity to her advantage. He told her that if she violated his injunction again, he would give her a long jail sentence.

When the trial was over, Mother Jones traveled to the southern West Virginia coal fields, where she worked on several local UMW strikes. She found that another judge had issued another injunction to keep her from speaking. She also found that the strike-related violence had increased. Miners were being shot and beaten. Storekeepers were told not to sell food to union members or their families. Despite the violence, Mother Jones and the other union organizers kept working, often in very dangerous situations. After their evening meetings, she said, "we sat through the night on the river bank. Frequently we would hear bullets whiz past us as we sat huddled between boulders, our black clothes making us invisible in the blackness of the night."

One night in a West Virginia town called Stanford Mountain, a group of armed men, led by the local deputy sheriff, killed eight striking miners as they slept. Hearing what had happened, Mother Jones hurried to Stanford Mountain the next day. She saw the murdered men still lying on their beds. She saw bullet holes in the walls of their shacks. She tried to comfort the crying wives and children of the murdered miners.

No one was ever punished for the murders on Stanford Mountain. The miners who lived were very scared by the shootings, too scared to continue the strike. Despite the hard work of Mother Jones and the other UMW organizers, the strike ended. But Mother Jones did not give up, vowing that someday the organizers would return to West Virginia and win the battle against the mining companies. She told a national meeting of the United Mine Workers in July 1902: "These fights must be won if it costs the whole country to win them. These fights against the oppressor and the capitalists, the ruling classes, must be won if it takes us all to do it."

Obviously, Mother Jones did not believe in giving up. Nor did she believe in compromise. Her uncompromising opinions were very different from the opinions of UMW president John Mitchell. The two had different ideas about how to deal with the coal companies. She wanted the miners to win better conditions by striking and causing a shortage of coal, and she believed that the union was strong enough to win such a strike. Mitchell, on the other hand, wanted to work with the coal companies to find a solution that everyone would like. He thought that the miners were too weak to win a strike and that the public would not support them if there was not enough coal that winter.

The two disagreed in public about the huge 1902 coal strike in Pennsylvania. The United Mine Workers had demanded union recognition, an eight-hour workday, and a 20 percent increase in pay. The strike began in May and soon involved about 147,000 mine workers in Pennsylvania. Mine operators and the big railroad companies, which actually controlled most of the coal companies, did not want to give in to the workers' demands. The strike dragged on. Concern grew since people in some parts of the United States depended upon this region's coal for heating their homes, and the fall's cold weather had begun. In October, President Theodore Roosevelt called on the coal companies to bargain with the striking miners. To get the companies to cooperate, President Roosevelt threatened to have the government take over the mines and use the U.S. Army to run them. Mitchell wanted to let an independent group set up the terms of the bargain. Mother Jones disagreed. She knew that the miners had worked hard on the strike. She thought that the workers themselves should make the bargain with the coal companies.

Since Mitchell was the UMW president, he made the final decision. He agreed to an independent group picked by President Roosevelt. The group settled the strike in favor of the miners. But Mother Jones was disappointed with the settlement, which did not recognize the union as the official voice representing and bargaining for the miners. Nor did it meet all the union demands. Instead of the 20 percent raise they had wanted, miners received a 10 percent increase. And most of the miners were granted a nine-hour, but not an eight-hour workday.

Mother Jones later wrote about how angry Mitchell's decision made her. Many miners, however, were glad to win the strike, even if they did not get everything they wanted. They called John Mitchell a great leader. There were parades in his honor. At a UMW meeting in 1903, union members talked about buying Mitchell a $10,000 house, to thank him for winning the strike. (This was at a time when the average coal miner earned about $520 a year.) They wrote a description of what they wanted to do. Mother Jones was the first to speak about the idea: "If John Mitchell can't buy a house to suit him for his wife and his family out of his salary, then I would suggest that he get a job that will give him a salary

John Mitchell, president of the United Mine Workers of America.

People line up for coal during the coal strike of 1902. Jones wanted the union to negotiate directly with the coal companies.

to buy a $10,000 house. Most of you do not own a shingle on the roof that covers you." Then she tore up the description and threw it on the ground.

Calmly, John Mitchell thanked the miners but did not accept their idea. He suggested instead that the $10,000 be used to build a memorial to miners killed in the most recent strike. Though he was angry inside, he did not mention Mother Jones's bitter speech. But the friendship between the union president and the opinionated old lady would never be the same.

CHAPTER SIX

The Crusade of the Mill Children

Ever since she had worked with little children in the cotton mills of Alabama, Mother Jones had a special concern for children who were forced to go to work. Jones realized that despite state laws against child labor, many thousands of children in the South and the North were working in factories and mills. In Pennsylvania there was a law against anyone under the age of 13 working in the cloth mills, where work was often dangerous. Fast-moving machines that wove thread into cloth could chop off a hand or a finger. The law said that children should not work around the dangerous machines. But no one enforced the Pennsylvania law against child labor. Mill owners were free to hire anyone they chose. Often they chose to hire children because children worked for much less pay than adults and for the same number of hours.

Mother Jones hated to see pale little children working from sunup to sundown. She thought that all children needed time to play in the sunshine and to go to school. Mother Jones spoke out against child labor. She once said, "Turn the jails into school rooms, take the children out of the mills and factories and sweatshops and allow them to develop their bodies and their minds." Mother Jones wanted a national law that would prevent child labor, and she wanted state governments to enforce the child labor laws that already existed. She looked for a way to get other people to notice the working children.

In May 1903, mill workers in the city of Philadelphia went on strike. The leaders of the mill workers' union, the Textile Workers Union, wanted a shorter workweek for adults and children. In Philadelphia, at least 16,000 children under 16 worked 10 hours a day, six days a week in the cloth mills. For their long week's work they were paid $2 or $3. For the same week's work, adults were paid $13.

Mother Jones went to the Textile Workers Union headquarters in Philadelphia. She wanted to help the strikers. Through the mill workers' union, she got to know some of the mill children in Philadelphia. Every day mill children who had been hurt at their jobs came into the union building. Some of the children were missing a hand; some were missing a thumb; some had broken fingers. Mother Jones said the children "were stooped little things, round shouldered and skinny."

Mother Jones wanted people to know about the sad state of the working children. She asked newspaper reporters why they did not write about the children who got hurt working in the cloth mills. The reporters told her that the mill owners also owned part of the newspapers. The mill owners would not allow their newspapers to print stories about the children.

Mother Jones had an idea: She decided that she herself would tell the stories of the mill children. She would do her best to get the public's attention and help the children. She organized a children's march. Many mill children gathered and walked through the city of Philadelphia from Independence Square to the City Hall. Outside City Hall, a crowd gathered to see the mill children. There were newspaper reporters in the crowd. Mother Jones made her way to the front and spoke to the people. She brought to the front of the crowd several children who had crushed hands and broken fingers from working with dangerous machinery in the cloth mills. Mother Jones held up the children's hands. That got the reporters' attention. She said, "Philadelphia's mansions were built on the broken bones, the quivering hearts and drooping heads of these children." The reporters wrote down what she said. The next day newspapers as far away as New York had stories about the march.

In July, Mother Jones had another idea. She told union leaders of her plan to organize another march against child labor. This march would go for 125 miles, from the city of Philadelphia all the way to President Theodore Roosevelt's summer home on Long Island. The striking mill workers liked the idea of the march, which they called the "Crusade of the Mill Children." More than 100 children got permission from their parents to join the march. Many adult mill workers decided to go, too.

On the afternoon of July 7, the group of 300 set out. An eight-year-old boy named Danny James led the procession, carrying a sign that said "We are Textile Workers." Two boys played a fife and drum. The rest of the children carried posters and waved flags. One poster read, "We Want to Go to School." Others read, "We Want Time to Play" and "More Schools, Less Hospitals."

Many of the marching children's bodies were deformed by the work they had done. James Ashworth was a 10-year-old boy whose back was stooped over like an old man's. His job in the mill was to carry bundles of yarn that weighed 75 pounds. For his work he was paid three dollars a week. Eddie Dunphy was 12 years old. For 11 hours each day, his job was to sit on a high stool and pass the right thread to another mill worker. He, too, was paid three dollars a week. Gussie Rangnew was a little girl who looked like an old woman. Her face was wrinkled and tired. Gussie spent the whole day packing stockings in a factory into boxes for shipment.

Crusade of the Mill Children. Mother Jones led a 1903 march of children to President Theodore Roosevelt's summer house.

The children sang and talked as they walked. They were very happy not to be working in the factories and mills. They liked the sunshine and the fresh air. Soon, however, it grew very hot. Some of the smaller children grew tired and were sent home. The rest followed the path of Philadelphia's Liberty Bell, which was being taken on a tour to New York City. The children carried tin cups and knapsacks. All along the way the children were greeted by reporters, well-wishers, and farmers who brought them fresh food. The group cooked in washtubs beside the road. Sometimes trainmen gave them free rides.

When the marchers came to a town, they stopped and held a meeting. They marched through New Jersey, stopping in Trenton and Princeton. When the marchers stopped in Princeton, they slept in a barn owned by former President Grover Cleveland. Other times they camped in tents they had brought along with them on the march.

They continued northeast through other towns including Hoboken and stopped just across the river from New York City. To enter the city, the group needed a parade permit from the mayor. The mayor of New York did not want to grant the permit and let the children come into the city. But Mother Jones convinced him that, as U.S. citizens, the children had the right to come into New York City. The children marched through the streets of New York. Thousands of people came out to see the "Crusade" marchers and to hear Mother Jones speak. The children had a great time. They spent a day swimming and playing in the East River. They toured the wild animal show that was being held at Coney Island, Brooklyn.

After their tour of New York, most of the marchers went back home. Mother Jones continued with three small boys, the oldest of whom was 11 years old. Mother Jones and the boys marched on to Oyster Bay, Long Island, more than 35 miles away. They went to the summer home of President Theodore Roosevelt. Mother Jones wanted to talk with him about child labor. She knew how the President loved children, how he romped and played with his own sons, and she thought that if the President saw these poor young boys and heard how hard they worked, he would surely pass a national law to protect them.

Mother Jones and the three boys arrived at the gate of the President's mansion. She spoke with the President's secretary. But the President, who was vacationing there, refused to see them. His secretary claimed that the President had nothing to do with child labor. He said that the matter was in the hands of the states and the Congress, not the President.

Still determined to get the boys to the President, she wrote letters to Roosevelt that were published in New York newspapers. But still he refused to see them. The President's secretary wrote back after the second letter. He said that there was nothing the President or the Congress could do. Angry and disappointed Mother Jones took the boys home to Philadelphia.

Later in her life, Mother Jones wrote about the crusade:

> We walked all the way to Oyster Bay from
> Philadelphia to see the man who was President of the
> United States . . . and he would not see us. He is a
> brave guy when he wants to take a gun and go out
> and fight other grown people, but when those chil-
> dren went to him he could not see them. . . . The
> young ones all went back strong and well, but they
> had to go into the mills again.

The Children's Crusade did not win a national child labor law. But it did make the newspapers write about child labor. Many reporters wrote about the sad lives and dangerous jobs of the mill children. Many people read the newspapers and learned about the children.

Public awareness and pressure led some state lawmakers to do something. Within a year of the crusade, Pennsylvania passed a stronger law to keep children out of factories until they were 14. New York and New Jersey also passed tougher laws. In 1916, Congress finally passed a national law against some kinds of child labor, but it was overturned by the Supreme Court in 1918. Not until 1938 did Congress pass a national child labor law that was upheld by the Supreme Court. So, in the early part of the 20th century, protection of children from harsh working conditions and long days of work still depended on state laws. Even then, enforcing the state laws was hard. Businesses found ways to get around the regulations, and poor families still needed extra money. Parents who needed the extra money to buy food lied about their children's ages so that they could go to work. Despite new state laws, many poor children continued to work in factories and mines.

CHAPTER SEVEN

Coal Miners Strike in Colorado

In 1858, three brothers from Georgia discovered gold in Colorado. Thousands of people began to move west, hoping to get rich. People discovered other valuable minerals in the earth— silver, copper, lead, and coal. Mining became a big business when the railroad arrived in Colorado in 1870, making it easier to move metals and coal. Many people moved to Colorado and got jobs as miners. The new miners in northern Colorado were mostly Irish, Welsh, Scottish, and English immigrants and Americans from other parts of the country. Most spoke English. In southern Colorado, however, many of the miners were Mexican, Greek, Italian, Hungarian, and Polish immigrants who had only recently come to the United States.

With the growth of the mining industry, miners' unions came to northern and southern Colorado. The United Mine Workers had many members in the north. The UMW and another union called the Western Federation of Miners, or WFM, which represented mostly metal miners, worked in southern Colorado.

Both the UMW and the WFM found it difficult to organize in southern Colorado, for three main reasons. First, many miners in the south spoke little English. Second, the southern coal fields were more isolated and harder to reach than those in the north. Many mines were located in steep canyons. Third, all of the coal mines in southern Colorado were owned by two powerful companies. One company, the Colorado Fuel and Iron Company (CF & I), was owned by millionaire industrialist John D. Rockefeller, Jr. Rockefeller made his fortune by pushing his competitors out of the oil business and forming a monopoly. Then he bought other industries, like the Colorado mines.

The other company, the Victor-American Company, was owned by another millionaire, Jay Gould. Gould had made his fortune in railroads and had worked against the striking railroad

Mother Jones tried to organize workers in mines owned by John D. Rockefeller Jr.'s Colorado Fuel and Iron Company.

workers in the Great Railway Strike of 1877. Both CF & I and Victor-American were very profitable and very strong companies whose owners and management disliked unions.

Despite the strength of these powerful companies, some miners began to join unions. Between 1880 and 1904, there were 13 coal- and metal-mining strikes in the state, many of which were organized to win an eight-hour workday for the miners.

In 1901, the Colorado state legislature passed a law saying that eight hours was the legal working day; if workers labored more than eight hours in one day, they had to be paid extra. But the state courts rejected the law, saying it interfered with employers' rights to make decisions about their workers. The next year the people of Colorado were given the chance to vote on whether or not they wanted the law. They voted in favor of an eight-hour-day law, but the new legislature, which had strong ties to the mining companies, would not pass another law.

The lack of a law to protect them made the miners in northern and southern Colorado angry, and they wanted to strike in protest. The unions had to decide whether or not to call a strike for an eight-hour workday. In 1903, the Western Federation of Miners was encouraging its members—miners of lead, zinc, and copper—to strike. The WFM asked the UMW to join the strike. UMW members wanted to strike, but UMW president John Mitchell preferred bargaining to strikes. Mitchell did not know what to do. He needed more information to make a decision. To help him decide, Mitchell sent Mother Jones to investigate conditions in southern Colorado, where miners were especially poor.

Mother Jones dressed as a peddler. She wore an old calico dress and carried a case full of fabric, pins and needles, and cutlery. She disguised herself so that she would be left alone. She did not want the coal companies to know that she was in Colorado. Mother Jones traveled throughout southern Colorado in October 1903. She met with the WFM leaders, who were beginning to ask coal miners to join their union. She visited with miners and their families, and she collected information so that she could report back to John Mitchell.

What she told Mitchell was shocking. She reported that the living and working conditions of the miners were terrible. She said that the miners lived like slaves to the coal companies. She saw children who did not get enough to eat and miners' tiny houses with dirt floors and broken windows. The coal companies owned the miners' one-room houses, and the companies could force the miners out of their houses at any time.

Instead of cash, the miners told her how they were paid in company scrip. As in other places, scrip could only be used to buy food, clothing, and mining tools at company stores, which had very high prices. Coal miners were paid by the weight of the minerals they dug. The weighing was done by the company, often with scales that short-weighted the amount. The miners had no right to weigh the coal themselves.

Mother Jones told John Mitchell about the miners' lives. After listing the miners' problems, Mother Jones recommended to Mitchell that he call a strike. Mitchell did not want to call a strike, but he had to respond to the reports he got from Jones and the other investigators. When he tried to set up a meeting with the mining companies, they refused, saying that the union did not represent their workers. Mitchell was left with no choice: On

November 9, 1903, Mitchell called the UMW strike in northern and southern Colorado.

Coal and metal miners moved out of their company-owned houses into tents provided by the union. Mother Jones worked among the striking miners in the southern part of the state, helping to pass out food, clothing, and medicine and holding meetings. She encouraged the strikers with her powerful words. Because she herself was an immigrant, the southern miners listened to her with respect and love.

The strike seemed to be working. No coal was dug out of the mountains. As the cold winter approached, people across the state began to notice a shortage of heating fuel. Citizens began to pressure the coal companies to give the miners what they wanted. Feeling this pressure from the public, the northern mining companies agreed to meet the union's demands. The mining companies agreed to give the northern miners an eight-hour workday, lawful weighing, and increased pay.

But the southern mining companies made no such agreement. The two powerful coal companies still refused to meet with the unions. UMW president John Mitchell thought that the southern miners would never be able to win their strike. He wanted to abandon the southern miners and settle the strike in the north. He knew that settling the dispute with employers in the north would leave the southern miners on their own, without an agreement. Nonetheless, he suggested that the northern miners should accept the companies' offer.

Mitchell's way of thinking made Mother Jones very angry. She thought the northern and southern miners should stick together and remain united in Colorado until all miners got what they needed. She thought Mitchell was giving up on the southern miners. Angrily she rushed to a union meeting in the north, where northern union members were voting on the agreement.

Mother Jones made an emotional speech to the northern miners. She told them that they would betray the southern miners if they accepted the proposed settlement. She said to them.

> Brothers, you English speaking miners of the north-
> ern fields promised your southern brothers, seventy

percent of whom do not speak English, that you
would support them to the end. Now you are asked
to betray them, to make a separate settlement. You
have a common enemy and it is your duty to fight to
a finish. Are you brave men? Can you fight as well as
you can work? I had rather fall fighting than working.
If you go back to work here and your brothers fall in
the south, you will be responsible for their defeat.

After hearing Mother Jones, the union members stood up and
cheered for her. Her powerful speech had convinced the northern miners. They voted overwhelmingly to continue the strike,
united with the southern miners.

UMW president Mitchell was furious with Mother Jones. He
kept trying to reach a settlement in the north. He told UMW
organizers to ask the northern miners to change their minds and
go back to work. After Mother Jones had gone back to help the
southern miners, he finally convinced the northern miners to
accept the settlement. On November 30, a week after Mother
Jones's speech, the northern union members voted again. This
time they decided to follow Mitchell and accept the contract
offered by the northern companies. The southern miners were
left on their own to continue their strike.

Mother Jones was disappointed and angry that the union had
given up on the strikers in southern Colorado. She was angry
about Mitchell's decision to settle for the northern miners. She
knew that Mitchell had left the southern miners on strike, without hope for their own agreement. By ending the strike in the
north, Mitchell had taken the public pressure off the coal companies. There would be no further coal shortage, which the southern strikers needed to win their demands.

Mother Jones saw the southern strikers living in tents through
the cold Colorado winter. At the same time, a satisfied Mitchell
was touring Europe, visiting union leaders there. She never for-
gave him for what she saw as neglecting and forgetting the workers. She would leave her UMW job soon after the end of the strike
in southern Colorado.

But right now she wanted to be with the miners in the south.

Mother Jones worked with the Western Federation of Miners in an area of Colorado called Cripple Creek. Bravely the miners continued their strike, despite the strikebreaking scabs who had been brought in from other states by the mining companies.

The winter of 1903-1904 was one of the coldest on record, and the miners suffered terribly. Without work, they could barely afford food on the 63 cents a week they got from the union. Many tied burlap sacks around their feet to keep them warm.

While the striking miners watched, strikebreakers working in the mines were protected by armed guards hired by the mining companies. These guards threatened strikers who came too close to the mines. They attacked strikers who walked alone. They even looted miners' tents and chased away their children. Finally the frustrated strikers began to arm themselves and fight back.

At the end of December, Governor James J. Peabody declared a state of martial law to protect the scabs in the southern mines. Under martial law, the government mobilized Colorado's state militia. Ordinary civilian rule was suspended. People's rights were taken away. Soldiers could enter houses or make arrests as they wished. Hundreds of strikers were arrested and detained outside in the snow and freezing temperatures.

Instead of being calmed by the enactment of martial law, soldiers and company guards became more and more vicious. Miners were shot as they slept. Union leaders were arrested and jailed. In jail they were not allowed to talk to anyone or have any visitors.

Mother Jones stayed with the miners, sleeping in their tents. She traveled over snowy roads, visiting and organizing. She was about 65 years old, and the exhausting work in Colorado was bad for her health. In late 1903, she got pneumonia and had to spend time in the hospital. During late January 1904, she stayed at a Socialist friend's home in Omaha, Nebraska, resting and getting her strength back.

Eagerly she returned to Colorado in February, going straight to the southern town of Trinidad, where the Western Federation of Miners had an office. Union miners came from the mines around Trinidad to hold meetings and make decisions about the strike. Mother Jones knew that, under martial law, soldiers were

Cripple Creek. Mine guards and Colorado's state militia protect strikebreakers during the violent 1903-1904 strike.

arresting union organizers, so she slept in her clothes just in case she was arrested at night. Sure enough, one Saturday night in March, soldiers burst into her hotel room and told her to come with them.

Three other organizers were arrested at the same time. They were all arrested by the Colorado militia, whom Mother Jones liked to call "lap dogs" because of their unquestioning obedience to the governor's commands. The soldiers put her on a train and told her that the governor wanted her to leave the state. Instead of leaving Colorado, she got a friendly train conductor to let her ride his train into Denver. There she wrote the governor an angry letter. She told him she was back in town. "I wish to notify you, governor, that you don't own the state," she wrote. "I am here in the capital," she continued, "what in the hell are you going to do about it?"

The governor was very angry at Mother Jones, but he did nothing. Defiantly, Mother Jones left Denver to go back to the miners. While the miners loved her for her independence and stubbornness, these same characteristics made her enemies in Colorado. Her enemies tried hard to make her look bad. They accused her of a secret past as the manager of houses of prostitution. They claimed that she had managed houses in Denver,

Omaha, Kansas City, Chicago, and San Francisco in the 1880s and 1890s. Calling her a troublemaker and an agitator, they said that she always liked to control things, to have power, which they thought was a terrible trait for a woman to have.

A Denver newspaper called *Polly Pry* printed the story about Mother Jones's past. The newspaper said that Mother Jones got rich from her "business" until her boyfriend left her. Then, said *Polly Pry*, Mother Jones started drinking heavily and spent $15,000. For her enemies, this story was a great way to stir up bad publicity about her. (Ten years later, in 1914, the story was repeated when the *Polly Pry* article was printed in the U.S. Congress journal, the *Congressional Record*. It was later discovered that the Denver author of the story worked for CF & I, Rockefeller's powerful mining company in southern Colorado. CF & I was one of Mother Jones's greatest enemies.)

Friends of Mother Jones refused to pay attention to the *Polly Pry* story, and Mother Jones herself never said anything about it in public. Probably she thought it was best to ignore her enemies. In private, she told a friend that the story came from an old friendship of hers with a Catholic woman in Chicago. The woman died and was refused burial in a Catholic cemetery because she had been a prostitute. Mother Jones wrote an angry letter to the local newspaper about the Catholic Church, and for doing this Mother Jones was accused of being a prostitute.

The *Polly Pry* story did not change the miners' opinion of her. She was still their much-loved "Mother." She returned to the mines, where she traveled, holding meetings and rallies, but her enemies kept close watch over her wherever she went.

When she went back to Trinidad in April 1904, the militia arrested her again, and again the soldiers told her to leave the state. This time she did leave, traveling to Helper, Utah, a little town about 150 miles over the Colorado-Utah border. In Helper, another strike was going on, and Mother Jones began to hold union meetings there. One day she was told that she had been exposed to smallpox, a dangerous disease, and quarantined by local police for several days in an isolated shack on the edge of town. She insisted there was no smallpox in the town. Probably it was an easy way for the local police to lock her up.

After police lifted the quarantine, Mother Jones returned to Trinidad in June. There was important news waiting for her there. Until then, the UMW had been sending money to the local southern unions to help them with the strike. Now she learned from the miners in Trinidad that John Mitchell had decided to cut off UMW support for the strikers. The Western Federation of Miners would remain committed, but the strikers were losing hope.

At the mines, the police and mine guards were becoming more violent. They arrested striking miners and threw them into bull pens, outdoor fenced-in areas where the miners were exposed to rain and snow. Many other miners were beaten and killed. The mining companies told store owners not to sell any goods to the striking miners. When the miners responded by setting up their own stores, soldiers broke in and looted them. They dumped kerosene on the miners' sacks of flour and sugar, poisoned the meat, and stole whatever they wanted.

In July, Mother Jones was arrested for the third time during the strike. Soldiers led her from her hotel at gunpoint. The miners were discouraged to see their "Mother" being led away with guns pointed at her. She was soon released, but the miners were discouraged and depressed by her arrest. By October 1904, the unhappy strikers could hold out no longer; they gave in and went back to work. At least 33 people had been killed during the strike, which proved for now that the mining companies were too powerful to defeat. Miners went back to their company houses and their long, hard days in the mines.

After the strike failed, the Victor-American Company and the Colorado Fuel and Iron Company brought in new immigrant miners to work in the southern coal fields. The companies chose immigrant workers because they had seen during the strike that people who had recently come to the United States were easier to control. Because they spoke little English, it was harder for the immigrants to explain to the American public the unfair things that the companies did. And it was harder for the miners' unions to organize workers who spoke different languages. At first, many immigrant miners were happy to have even bad jobs. But the situation in Colorado was so bad that, 10 years later, even these immigrant miners would be ready to strike.

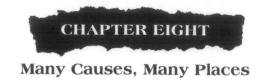

CHAPTER EIGHT

Many Causes, Many Places

The actions of the United Mine Workers during the Colorado miners' strike led Mother Jones to resign from her job with the UMW in 1904. Although she had lost faith in that union, she still believed in the cause of the miners. She vowed to fight for them, and she encouraged them to organize themselves. "Boys, get together and organize," she told a group of miners in Michigan. "It will make business better for your city. It will end the troubles. It will end the strikes. Down in Illinois they used to have strikes right along, but since the men organized they get together with the mine operators and talk over the matter and arrive at a decision as to their best interests. They never have any trouble there."

After she left the UMW, Jones spent several years as a lecturer for the Socialist Party of America. The Socialist party was a small party. But when Eugene V. Debs ran for U.S. President on the Socialist party ticket in 1904, he did manage to win 400,000 votes. (In 1920, he got 915,000 votes.) Mother Jones traveled through Montana, Missouri, Texas, Arizona, and the Indian Territory (which is now Oklahoma). She gave speeches about socialism and the rights of workers. Crowds that gathered to hear her applauded loudly when she spoke:

> Whether you know it or not, this is the last great fight of man against man. We are fighting for the time when there will be no master and no slave. When the fight of the workers to own the tools with which they toil is won, for the first time in human history man will be free.

When she was not giving lectures for the Socialist party, she worked for the railroad workers, helping them win recognition of their union by the railroad companies and the right to collective bargaining. Collective bargaining allows the union to settle differences between the workers and their employers. Instead of making a bargain and setting the terms of work, like hours and wages, with each individual worker, the companies recognized that the union represented all the workers and could settle the terms for them all. The right to collective bargaining was a big improvement for the railroad workers because it allowed them to settle differences with their employers peacefully, rather than through violent protests and strikes.

Other workers were not as lucky as the railroad workers. In 1904 and 1905 unemployment was the highest it had been since 1899, and there were many more workers than jobs. Workers who had jobs were afraid of losing them. To keep their jobs, workers had to do whatever factory owners and bosses told them. Many workers had hard, unhappy lives. Most Americans still began to work at the age of 14, and many people went to work at an even younger age.

Some labor leaders believed that American workers needed a new kind of help to make their lives better and to gain more control over their jobs. In January 1905, radical labor leaders called a secret meeting in Chicago to decide how workers could organize so they would have more control over the country's industries. The meeting's organizers wanted to make big changes in the way industry worked. They wanted workers to own industry themselves, so that they could participate in making decisions about their work. Mother Jones was invited to this meeting by William D. ("Big Bill") Haywood, a miner and union organizer for the Western Federation of Miners. Mother Jones had known Big Bill Haywood for over a year, having first met him during the 1903-1904 strike in Colorado.

Because of his union organizing during the Colorado strike, Haywood was badly beaten up by the state militia in Denver. After that strike, Haywood began to believe that unions for specific groups of workers, like the UMW and the WFM, could never be strong enough to help working people. Most unions at that time were for a small group of skilled workers, like carpenters or cigar makers, but most workers were employed in factories tending machines. Often these unskilled workers did not have a union to turn to. Haywood's idea and the idea of the other meeting organizers, was that all different kinds of workers—skilled and unskilled—needed to get together in one big union that would include all working people as members.

At the meeting were 27 Socialists, radical labor leaders, and reporters. Mother Jones was the only woman among them. Together they wrote a statement that called for a bigger meeting, where they would organize a single union for all workers. They issued a statement that included the following:

> The working class and the employing class have
> nothing in common. There can be no peace so long
> as hunger and want are found among millions of
> working people, and the few, who make up the
> employing class, have all the good things of life.

Mother Jones was in Chicago for the second meeting in June 1905. The meeting of 186 delegates lasted for two weeks. During the meeting, members of many unions and workers' groups started the new union called the Industrial Workers of the World—IWW for short. Members of the IWW became known as "Wobblies." The Wobblies had a big goal—to organize all workers of any industry, race, or nationality into "One Big Union." They invited every worker in the country to join what they called industrial democracy.

Mother Jones was there at the beginning of the IWW. So was her friend Eugene V. Debs, a leading Socialist. Lucy Parsons, the wife of a labor leader who had been hanged for the Haymarket bombing in Chicago, was at the meeting, too.

Mother Jones played only a small role in the meeting of the Wobblies. She did not give fiery speeches or lead demonstrations. Mother Jones was glad that the radical labor leaders started the IWW because she realized the importance of making deep changes in the way industry was organized. But she did not like to sit still while the leaders discussed and argued about their ideas. Mother Jones liked to be active and independent, and she was ready to get back to the workers and the everyday struggles that would bring about larger changes.

Until World War I, the Wobblies were an exciting and very active group whose membership grew to 250,000 workers. They reached out to the poorest workers and to those who had no union. They worked for higher wages, safer workplaces, and fair treatment of workers. They fought to defend the right to free speech so that radical organizers could speak to workers without being arrested. But at the same time, the Wobblies favored conflict more than collective bargaining and wanted a huge general strike that would overthrow the capitalist system. Debs and some of the other Socialists and radical leaders eventually left the IWW. The Western Federation of Miners withdrew from IWW membership in 1907.

Because she had other strong interests, Mother Jones lost contact with the Wobblies and their work about six months after the IWW was formed. But she did not lose touch with Big Bill Haywood. The next time she saw him he was in jail, accused of killing the former governor of Idaho.

In 1899, Idaho had been the site of a violent strike by lead and silver miners, who were members of the Western Federation of Miners. Governor Frank Steunenberg allowed the mining companies to bring in scabs to replace the strikers. The governor used soldiers to guard the scabs as they worked, and he ordered the arrests of many strikers. Because of these actions, he was hated by Idaho's working people, especially after the strike was lost.

Several years after the strike, Frank Steunenberg was no longer governor. One December day in 1905, the former Idaho governor walked out of his house. As he opened his front gate, a bomb exploded and killed him. Police said they tried to find out who had planted the bomb. Some weeks later, three union organizers were seized by armed private detectives in the Colorado night and put aboard a special train. The train took the three men to Idaho, where they were charged with the former governor's murder.

One of the three men was Big Bill Haywood. As soon as Mother Jones read the news, she got on a train and went to Idaho. Big Bill was her friend, and she was sure he had nothing to do with the bomb that had killed the governor. She was sure, too, that he was being falsely accused of the governor's murder.

The three men arrested in Colorado were all labor leaders who had worked with the Western Federation of Miners. Steunenberg had used brutal tactics during the WFM strike in Idaho, and WFM members were angry with him. But Mother Jones did not believe that their anger would have led them to murder.

The state of Idaho based its charge of murder on the statements of a man named Harry Orchard, who confessed to planting the bomb that killed Governor Steunenberg. He said that Big Bill Haywood and the other leaders of the WFM had ordered him to plant the bomb. The state of Idaho believed Harry Orchard, but hardly anyone else did. Orchard himself had confessed to murdering 18 people. Many people believed that the state had

William D. ("Big Bill") Haywood, seated at the right, at his 1907 trial. Mother Jones collected money for his defense.

convinced Orchard to testify against the WFM, in order to hurt the union. The current governor of Idaho, as well as President Theodore Roosevelt, disapproved of the WFM, because they thought it used violent methods and refused to cooperate with government. President Roosevelt called Haywood and the other defendants "undesirable citizens."

Mother Jones spent over a year traveling around the country, making speeches in support of the accused men and collecting money for their defense; several other labor organizations also supported the three men. The trial of the three union men started in January 1907. With the money raised by Mother Jones and others, the accused men hired Clarence Darrow, the most famous and respected trial lawyer in the country, to defend them. Darrow proved Harry Orchard's statement to be false. The three men were found not guilty by the jury, and they were freed. Mother Jones had helped save the union men from jail.

Never one to stay in one place for long, Mother Jones moved on to another place where workers were having problems. This time it was Westmoreland County, Pennsylvania, where she spent the late summer of 1908 with a group of striking miners. Mother Jones visited with the wives of the strikers in a town called Greensburg. She told the women to take their babies with them to the picket lines outside the mine. The women listened to Mother Jones. With their babies in their arms, the protesting women shouted at the scabs who were working in the mine.

The women were arrested for disturbing the peace. They took their babies with them to court. Since they could not afford bail money, a judge sent the women to jail. Again Mother Jones told the women what to do. She told them to sing to their babies all night long. If some women grew tired and could not sing any more, she said, others should continue the singing. Again the women listened to Mother Jones. They sang so loudly and so long that they began to disturb the people in nearby houses and hotels. After five days of singing, they were released from jail. Like the women who guarded mine entrances with brooms and frying pans, these women had learned from Mother Jones how to get what they wanted without violence.

Mother Jones moved on, to find another group of people in

Besides working to achieve a better life for American workers, Mother Jones also helped Mexicans gain political rights.

need. In the years from 1907 to 1911, she spent a great deal of time raising money for Mexican revolutionaries. It was a coincidence that got her involved in this work. She was in Arizona in June 1907 to organize copper miners for the Western Federation of Miners. On June 30, she met a Mexican man named Manuel Sarabia, who worked for a local Spanish-language newspaper.

Later that day, while she was giving a speech to the copper miners, Sarabia was kidnapped on the streets of Douglas, Arizona. He was forced into a car and taken across the border into Mexico. Once in Mexico, he was taken by police on a five-day mule trip and put in prison. Friends of Sarabia's found Mother Jones and told her about the kidnapping. She learned more about what had happened. Since 1875, Mexico had been governed by a cruel dictator, President Porfirio Díaz, who had taken away the freedoms and rights of the Mexican people. There were many Mexican people who were unhappy with Díaz and wanted a new president.

Sarabia was a leader of the Liberal party, a political party that was working to overthrow the Mexican president. While still in Mexico, Sarabia had publicly called Díaz a dictator. For that Sarabia had spent a year in a Mexican jail. When he was released from jail, Sarabia came to the United States to continue to fight against the Mexican dictator. He thought he would be safer in the United States, but he was wrong. He had been kidnapped in Arizona at the request of Díaz.

Once Mother Jones knew Sarabia's story, she got angry. She led a local protest march. She encouraged everyone to send telegrams of protest to President Theodore Roosevelt. The protests worked—eight days after he was kidnapped, the Mexican police returned Sarabia to American authorities.

Sarabia and his revolutionary friends were exiles, afraid to return to Mexico. If they went back to Mexico, they would be captured and killed. From Sarabia and his friends, Jones learned of their efforts to overthrow President Porfirio Díaz. Many of Sarabia's friends were in jail in the United States, accused of violating U.S. neutrality laws. These laws made it illegal for anyone in the United States to work with political movements in other countries. But while Sarabia's friends were in jail for their political work, supporters of Díaz were allowed to work freely in the United States. It was these Díaz supporters who had kidnapped Sarabia in Arizona.

Mother Jones knew how she could help Sarabia and his revolutionary friends. She traveled all over the country, making speeches about the Mexican men. She raised thousands of dollars to get lawyers for the Mexican revolutionaries who had been jailed in the United States. She met with newly elected President William Howard Taft and asked him to pardon the Mexican revolutionaries. On June 14, 1910, she testified before Congress about them. She asked Congress to learn more about these Mexican prisoners and to protect them. She said that it was the duty of the United States, as the "cradle of liberty," to help people of other countries who were trying to gain their freedom. "Gentlemen," she told members of Congress, "in the name of our own Revolutionary heroes, in the name of the heroes unborn, in the name of those whose statues stand silently there in Statuary Hall, I beg that this body of representatives will protect these Mexican men from the tyranny and oppression of that bloody tyrant, Díaz."

From prison, the Mexican exiles wrote to thank Mother Jones for her work to help them. "You are setting a noble example," they wrote, "and teaching a lesson humanity should not forget. You, an old woman, are fighting with indomitable [unyielding] courage; you, an American, are devoting your life to free Mexican slaves."

The congressional hearings lasted five days. When the hearings were over, the Mexican men were freed. By May 1911, Porfirio Díaz was losing power. He resigned the presidency and fled to Europe. After the Mexican dictator left, a new democratic government was set up, and in October 1911, Mother Jones traveled to Mexico. She went with the vice president of the United Mine Workers to meet with the new Mexican president, Francisco Madero. They hoped to be able to help organize Mexican miners.

President Madero told his visitors that the new Mexican government would allow unions. This was the first time in Mexican history that union organizing had been allowed. Mother Jones called it "the greatest concession ever granted to anyone representing the laboring class of any nation." The Mexican people were thankful for the important work that Mother Jones had done for them. Wherever she went in Mexico during that trip, crowds gathered to see her. They yelled and cheered for her and sang songs to her.

Even while helping Mexican revolutionaries, Mother Jones did not forget the struggles of workers in the United States. Back in the United States, Mother Jones went wherever she was needed. In 1910 she worked to organize the brewery workers in Milwaukee, Wisconsin. Young girls worked in the beer breweries as bottle washers. They worked long days in wet clothes and wet shoes with the smell of sour beer all around them. Many of the girls got sick from spending the whole day cold and wet. The girls had to lift heavy cases of empty and full beer bottles weighing up to 150 pounds.

The girls were watched closely by their bosses. If they spent too much time in the bathroom, the bosses cursed and threatened them. For all their hard work, the girls were paid between 75 and 85 cents a day. They were not allowed to work more than three or four days a week. The girls were poor and needed the money they made from each day of work. They grew very scared if the bosses threatened to cut back the number of days they worked.

Mother Jones investigated the work conditions at the beer breweries. She visited the girls and learned about their work. Then she decided that something needed to be done to help the brewery workers, so she started to organize the girls into a union. She wrote a number of articles about the low wages and poor conditions in the breweries.

Mother Jones got other unions to help the brewery workers. She convinced the UMW to pass a rule against UMW members drinking Milwaukee beer. That scared the owners and managers of the beer brewing companies because they knew that miners were good customers. If the miners stopped drinking Milwaukee beer, it would hurt the brewing companies' business.

The brewing company owners listened to Mother Jones. Within months, the Pabst and Schlitz brewing companies recognized the new women's union. Once again Mother Jones had shown how workers' solidarity was a useful union tool. The union made a big difference, winning the girls much higher wages and better working conditions. It was one of Mother Jones's biggest—and most peaceful—successes.

CHAPTER NINE

"Her Boys" in West Virginia

Mother Jones came back to the UMW in 1911, after John Mitchell resigned. She traveled back and forth across the country meeting with striking miners and inspiring them to keep up their strikes. As she visited 14 states and covered 15,000 miles, she told strikers, "There is no such thing as fail. We have got to win."

Mother Jones continued to make many speeches. In her late seventies, she was still a commanding speaker. Her speeches were advertised in the local newspapers as well as with flyers passed out on the streets, and many people came out to hear her. Whenever and wherever she appeared, crowds cheered, stamped their feet, and clapped their hands when they heard her name. Women blew kisses at her and threw flowers at her feet. Usually, when she finished speaking she passed a hat around the audience to collect money for strikers. Mother Jones often convinced people to give all the money they had with them.

In the spring of 1912, she headed west to help with a strike of western railroad workers against the Pacific Northwest Railroad. She was in Montana with striking copper workers when she learned that a strike in the West Virginia coal mines had begun in April 1912.

The coal mines in southern West Virginia produced a great deal of coal. Strikes of coal miners in other parts of the country could be broken more easily if nonstriking coal miners in West Virginia kept working and producing cheap coal to sell nationwide. Getting West Virginian coal miners to join the union and getting the coal companies to recognize the union were important national goals for union leaders.

Mother Jones decided to go to West Virginia to be with "her boys." She liked to "travel light," so she wrapped up her few possessions in a black shawl and took a train from Montana to West Virginia. The strike was in Paint Creek and Cabin Creek. There were no unions in Cabin Creek, but Mother Jones knew the Paint Creek miners from her earlier work in West Virginia. She had convinced them to join the UMW in spite of the danger, and she was proud of these union miners.

Paint Creek and Cabin Creek each carved a narrow valley on opposite sides of a high, steep mountain ridge. In some places there was only enough room in the valleys for a set of railroad tracks and a road. A fight over their contract had led thousands of union coal miners on the Paint Creek side to strike. While they were not yet ready to strike, the Cabin Creek miners across the ridge were also tired of their employers' oppressive policies. Mother Jones did not know it when she arrived in West Virginia in July 1912, but the Paint Creek–Cabin Creek strike would become one of the bloodiest strikes in American history.

National Guard troops prepare weapons during the 1912 Paint Creek–Cabin Creek strike in West Virginia.

The situation of the miners in the Creek district seemed to Mother Jones even worse than the last time she had been in West Virginia. In Cabin Creek, armed guards patrolled the roads, which were owned by the coal companies. People were not allowed on the roads unless they could give a good reason why they were there. Miners were paid in scrip and charged high rents for the tiny shacks where they lived. They had to pay high taxes for schools, doctors, and even burial. The miners were paid by the carload of coal. Mining companies could pay them less by building wooden cribs and attaching them to the sides of each freight car. This was called "cribbing." By cribbing, each car could hold much more coal, but the miners were still paid the same amount.

When the Cabin Creek miners joined the strike, many were kicked out of their company-owned houses. The UMW set up a tent colony for the strikers in Holly Grove, about 15 miles from the state capital of Charleston. There were other tent colonies in other parts of the state.

The coal companies hired guards from the well-known Baldwin-Felts detective agency, which specialized in providing armed guards to protect company property and strikebreakers during strikes. The Baldwin-Felts guards set up machine guns aimed at the miners' tents. They kept striking miners from leaving their tent colonies. They kicked miners off trains and kept them from crossing company-owned bridges.

The Baldwin-Felts guards began to attack the tent colonies with machine guns. The guards killed and wounded many miners and members of their families. While the main demand of the miners' strike was originally the conditions of a new contract, the removal of these Baldwin-Felts guards soon became their most urgent concern.

Mother Jones arrived in Charleston, West Virginia, in July 1912. Right away she began to meet with the striking miners. The strikers came from the strike zone to see her, and Mother Jones pledged to stay with the strikers as long as they needed her. She inspired the striking miners, telling them that they would win the strike. Among the strikers' major demands were union recognition, an end to the brutal system of mine guards, the hiring of miner-paid workers to check the weight of the coal, and higher pay. The coal miners also demanded payment in money, not company scrip, every two weeks, and the right not to be forced to buy in company stores.

Mother Jones knew that the miners were scared of the armed company guards. She encouraged them to be brave. "I want to say," she told the miners, "they will not be able to get an army in the United States big enough to crush us." She told the miners that they needed to protest against the mining companies. In Montgomery, West Virginia, a town just outside the strike zone, she spoke to mine workers gathered in a baseball park. "My friends, you are exploited, you are robbed, you are plundered. You have submitted to it, you haven't protested. You grunt but you don't fight as you ought to do."

Mother Jones was warned several times not to enter the strike zone. Miners and police told her that she would be killed if she tried to go into the dangerous zone. But the warnings did not stop her. "I am going to talk Sunday at Paint Creek. They said that if I went up there last Sunday they were going to riddle me with bullets. Now, I went, and there wasn't a bullet struck me. I am going next Sunday."

True to her word, Mother Jones went to Paint Creek. She found a quiet, heavily guarded town. She talked with the miners and their families, some of whom were still living in company houses. From them she learned firsthand about the brutality they were suffering from the guards.

One little boy told Mother Jones how the guards had chased his father away. No one knew where his father had gone. Then the guards had thrown his mother and his brothers and sisters out of their house and had beaten them all. When Mother Jones looked under the boy's shirt, she saw that his shoulders were black and blue with bruises from the beatings.

Mother Jones saw that the strikers' lives were being threatened, and she realized that the miners needed to protect themselves from the armed guards. At other times in her life she had spoken out against violence and used creative means of nonviolent protest. Now she thought that the men needed guns. "If you haven't got good guns, buy them," she told them. Some miners joined the National Rifle Association and were able to buy low-cost government surplus guns.

Mother Jones claimed to be 80 years old. Her hair was pure white, but her age did not slow her down. Other union organizers reported that she could walk for miles and miles through the mountainous coal country and never show signs of being tired.

At the beginning of August 1912, she decided to go across the ridge to Cabin Creek, to visit the miners there, who were striking even though they were not part of the union. She took the train to Eskdale, a town along the creek. In all the other towns along Cabin Creek, the companies had guards patrolling the streets. Eskdale was the only town in the area that was not controlled by the mining companies. She would be allowed to speak there.

A small group of Cabin Creek miners not yet on strike showed up to hear her speak. At the end of her strong speech, the men wanted to join the union. When the miners finished the union pledge, making them members of the union, Mother Jones told them to go back to their jobs. She told them to say nothing about having joined the union. She knew there would be trouble for them if the mining company found out they had joined.

But the company did find out. There had been a company spy at the meeting. He reported to the company the names of each of the men who had joined the union. The next day, the new union men all were fired.

On August 13, 1912, Mother Jones held her second meeting in Eskdale. After that meeting, some miners from another town came up to her. They told her that there were other men in their town who wanted to join the union. The other men had been afraid to come to her meeting. The miners asked Mother Jones to come to the Red Warrior mining camp and speak to them. She agreed.

The miners and Mother Jones started to walk to the Red Warrior camp. The miners walked along the railroad tracks, which were owned by the mining company. She traveled along the dry creek bottom, which was the only part of the land not owned by the mining companies. The companies could not arrest her for trespassing if she was in the creek.

On the way to the camp, she met up with a group of armed

guards standing along the creek beside a machine gun. The guards pointed the machine gun at the group of miners accompanying her. Unafraid, Mother Jones approached the guards and put her hand over the muzzle of the gun. She spoke to the guard who stood closest to the machine gun. "Young man, I want to tell you that if you shoot one bullet out of this gun at those men, if you touch one of my white hairs, that creek will run with blood, and yours will be the first to crimson it. . . . These boys have no guns! Let them pass!"

She told the guards that there were 500 armed miners hiding in the mountains around them. She said that if the guards fired on her, the hidden miners would shoot them all. The guards let the group pass. Of course, there were no armed miners in the mountains, but the guards did not know that. Once again, Mother Jones had bluffed her way through a dangerous situation.

Another time she held a strike meeting on a public road. Company guards came and told her to stop the meeting, but Mother Jones said that public roads were owned by the citizens. She said that as a citizen she was part owner of the road and had the right to talk there. She was so persuasive that again the company guards were afraid to shoot.

Once she was on her way to a meeting in Wineberg when she was stopped by armed guards who told her that the area was owned by the mining company. The only way she could go to her meeting, they said, was to walk in the creek bed, which was full of cold, rushing water. The guards were sure that this dainty old lady would not try to walk through the freezing water. Surprising them, Mother Jones took off her shoes, held up her skirt and waded into the water. She walked in the cold creek water all the way to the meeting. She even stood in the water as she led the meeting. It was brave and selfless acts like this that made Mother Jones the "angel of the miners."

Mother Jones organized the striking miners from Paint Creek and Cabin Creek in a march to the state capital. She led a group of 1,000 strikers who were hoping to meet with the governor. When the group arrived in Charleston, Mother Jones made a speech on the steps of the state capitol building. She spoke for an hour and a half, demanding that Governor William E. Glasscock remove the armed mine guards. Mother Jones blamed the governor for the strike's violence. She said that he could control or even ban the Baldwin-Felts guards if he wanted to. But instead, she said, he was siding with the mining companies. She called him a coward. The governor ignored Mother Jones's speech and the miners' demands. But the miners listened and grew angry. The speech had reminded them of why they were striking. The speech also reminded the miners why they loved courageous Mother Jones so much.

As much as she was loved by the miners, she was hated by the coal company owners and operators because she had power over the miners. Her words could convince them to strike, or to fight, or to give their lives if necessary. "She comes into a State where peace and progress reign," said an enemy of hers. "She crooks her finger—20,000 contented men lay down their tools and walk out." A company lawyer called her "the most dangerous woman in America." Someone wrote a poem about how the company officials felt about her:

> How they fear her, how they hate her—hate her kind
>   and timeworn face.
> How they rush armed mobs to meet her when she
>   moves from place to place.

The mining companies continued to ignore the miners' demands. They hired scabs who were protected by the armed guards. Finally, miners throughout the Creek district could wait no longer, and they began to fight back. They hid in the mountains and shot at company guards. By the end of August, there were shootings almost every night. Sometimes people were shot during the day, too.

The increasing violence convinced the governor to act. At the end of September, he came to the strike zone and declared martial law. He brought in 1,200 state militia soldiers, who raided the miners' camps, taking all the weapons they could find. Hundreds of rifles, pistols, and daggers were taken from the miners. But the miners did not surrender all their weapons. They hid some of their guns in the woods. The governor told the soldiers to take weapons from the company guards, too. The soldiers took illegal dumdum bullets from the company guards. When these bullets struck a person, the bullets expanded, causing large jagged wounds. The company guards had used these bullets to fire on the striking miners.

With the state militia soldiers present, there was less violence in the strike zone. But in October 1912, the soldiers were ordered to withdraw from the strike zone. Now without jobs, many of the soldiers accepted positions as armed guards for the companies. The companies also began to bring in scabs from other parts of the country.

The situation of the strikers grew worse. Jones decided that the strike needed national publicity. She went on a speaking tour, telling the striking miners' story in Ohio and Washington, D.C. She talked to politicians and reporters about the violence being used by the company guards against strikers.

While she was gone, the mining companies started a horrible new practice. They fitted a train with strong iron armor and machine guns. They sent the armored train through the mining towns and shot the machine guns at strikers' camps as the train sped by. They called the train the "Bullmoose Special."

On the night of February 7, 1913, the "Bullmoose Special" pulled into a tent colony at Holly Grove while strikers and their families were sleeping. Bullets ripped through the tents. Men, women, and children were shot as they slept. One miner was killed, but no one was arrested for the shootings. The shooting made the strikers even angrier, and they fought back. A group of miners surrounded a camp of company guards during the night. When the guards woke up and began to make their breakfast, the miners opened fire. The strikers killed at least 13 of the hated guards.

The increasingly desperate miners asked Mother Jones to explain their case to Governor Glasscock. On February 12, 1913, she took a delegation to see the governor. But on the way to the state capital, she was arrested, put in a car, and driven to the martial-law zone. Five union miners were also arrested. The entire group was tried by a military court in the martial-law zone. Mother Jones and the five miners protested, saying that it was illegal for the military court to try them, since they were civilians and had not been arrested in the martial-law zone. They thought they should be tried by a regular court. They refused to say anything in their own defense. But both the governor and the military court ignored their protest.

The trial continued and Mother Jones and the others were convicted and sentenced to a jail term. Few court records have survived, so it is impossible to know for sure what the charges were against Jones. She later claimed that she was charged with stealing a cannon and blowing up railroad tracks and sentenced to five years in jail. She was probably also charged with helping to commit murder, since she had told the miners to arm themselves and to fight back against the armed guards. Mother Jones was not surprised by the conviction. She knew that the military court was controlled by the mining companies. "Your judges are owned and controlled by the ruling class. You need not expect any justice in the courts; I don't."

But Mother Jones was never sent to jail. Instead, she was kept under guard in a private house in the martial-law zone. She was kept in one room for almost three months. She slept on a mattress on the floor and had to go out on a porch to wash her face. Eventually she grew sick with pneumonia.

While she was kept in the house, she managed to send out a number of letters and telegrams. With a friendly guard, she set up a system for smuggling letters out of her guarded room through a hole in the floor. When she hit two beer bottles against each other, the soldier knew to come. He crawled under the house and peeked up through the hole in the floor. She handed him a letter or telegram to deliver.

She sent letters and telegrams to powerful people she knew. In May, she sent one telegram to Senator John W. Kern of Indiana. She convinced him to ask the U.S. Senate to investigate the conditions in the coal fields of West Virginia. Senator Kern read her telegram to the entire Senate:

> From out of the military prison wall of Pratt, West
> Virginia, where I have walked over my eighty-fourth
> milestone in history, I send you the groans and tears

and heartaches of men, women and children as I
have heard them in this state. From out of these
prison walls, I plead with you for the honor of the
nation, to push that investigation, and the children
yet unborn will rise and call you blessed.

Mother Jones's telegrams got the attention of the public. The
office of the newly elected West Virginia governor, Henry D.
Hatfield, was flooded with questions and protests from all over
the country. Under pressure, Governor Hatfield started bargaining between the union miners and the mining companies. He
dismissed the sentences given to Mother Jones and the other
union organizers by the military court. At the end of May, after
nearly three months in solitary confinement, Mother Jones was
finally freed.

In the spring of 1913, UMW leaders and the coal operators
reached an agreement that included a nine-hour workday and
the workers' right to choose the people who weighed the coal.
But the miners were angry that the UMW leaders had not convinced the companies to agree to more of their demands. The
strike continued. By July 1913, after more than a year of bloody
violence, the strike finally paid off. The Paint Creek and Cabin
Creek miners won many of their demands including recognition
of their union by the mining companies. The union grew from
2,000 to 5,000 members. And Mother Jones became even more
well known and well loved by the miners.

CHAPTER TEN

Colorado, The Second Time

Colorado's government had passed laws to protect the miners, but the mining companies were so powerful that they ignored the laws, and state officials dared not punish the companies. Colorado state laws ordered twice monthly paydays for miners, checkweighmen (to prevent miners from being cheated), the right to form unions, the eight-hour workday, and payment in cash—not scrip. Because these laws were not enforced, the miners still suffered miserable conditions with little hope of union recognition. The miners in northern Colorado had gone on a short strike late in 1910, and the UMW had sent Mother Jones to the region in the winter of 1911. Although she believed that the strike could not be won without a strike of the southern miners at the same time, she had gone to northern Colorado and organized anyway. She had encouraged the striking miners to hold out against the Northern Coal and Coke Company. But the strike had quickly been broken by the mining company.

Mother Jones continued to hope that the northern and southern miners would strike together. That finally happened in 1913. The gains made by the northern miners in the 1903-1904 strike had been taken away. The conditions of the miners in the south were as bad as ever. With the support of the UMW, northern and southern Colorado miners went on strike in September.

Mother Jones had gone to Colorado before the strike was called to organize mine workers against Rockefeller's Colorado Fuel and Iron Company. CF & I owned 27 mining camps in southern Colorado and produced 40 percent of the coal dug in the state. CF & I treated miners very poorly. The company weighed the coal dishonestly, so the miners were paid too little. They were still paid in scrip, even though there was a law against it. There were many dangerous accidents in the mines. CF & I had brought in immigrant miners at the end of the 1903-1904 strike, and now only about a third of the southern miners spoke English. If many men who spoke the same language worked in the same mine, CF & I moved the men around so that the miners could not communicate with each other. This was a good way for the powerful coal company owners and managers to prevent worker solidarity.

The mining companies still did not like unions or union organizers. About 1,200 miners across Colorado were fired in 1912 for having joined the UMW. Mine guards kept union organizers from entering company towns, and if a union organizer was found in a company town, the mine guards often beat him and threw him out. So Mother Jones visited the company towns quietly. She sat on mounds of earth with miners as they ate their lunches. She visited with women as they bent over washtubs. She gave candy to the children.

The miners and their families lived in horrible houses. One family she met had to get under the bed every time it rained to stay dry. Some families could not afford clothes, so they dressed their children in burlap sacks. Mother Jones saw how the soot and dust from the mines killed all the grass and flowers in the town. She saw the company guards, armed with machine guns and rifles. She watched as the guards prevented miners from leaving their towns.

Mother Jones was being watched, too. When she went to the United Mine Workers' headquarters in Trinidad, Colorado, in September 1913, she immediately began receiving threatening letters. Someone drew a skull and crossbones on a photograph of her. She was followed everywhere by detectives hired by the mining companies. She saw some of the same brutal Baldwin-Felts guards who had worked for mining companies in West Virginia. The guards had been sent to Colorado to protect the mine owners' property. They brought with them the same machine guns and armored vehicles they had used in West Virginia.

The strike was called throughout the state on September 23, 1913. Eight to ten thousand miners left the mines. Since everything in the mining towns—streets, houses, stores, churches, bars, schools—was owned by the mining companies, the UMW quickly set up 12 tent colonies on land rented just outside company property. In cold rain, the striking miners moved their sparse belongings and their families out of the company houses.

The miners and their families were hurried off mine property by the Baldwin-Felts guards who had been hired by the company. Carrying all their possessions through the rain and mud, they moved into tents just as the fall and winter cold came. In spite of the cold weather, the strikers and their families liked life in the tent colonies. They felt freer than they ever had living in the company towns. They played baseball during the day and played accordions and guitars in the evenings. The women visited and cared for each other's children.

The families felt good about the strike. Whole mining families joined in the strike effort. The men carried signs and picketed, and the women and children sang union songs. One union song went as follows:

> We will win the fight today, boys.
> We'll win the fight today,
> Shouting the battle cry of union;
> We will rally from the coal mines,
> Shouting the battle cry of union.
> The union forever, hurrah boys, hurrah!
> Down with the Baldwins, up with the law;
> For we're coming Colorado, we're coming all the way,
> Shouting the battle cry of union.

Although she wasn't feeling well, Mother Jones made encouraging speeches to the miners. She could hold an audience's attention for two hours at a time. After her speeches, she listened to the miners' stories of strike-related violence. She heard how women and children were beaten by the company guards. She heard how soldiers wrecked the home and frightened the children of an undertaker who had buried two union miners. She heard how the miners were unfairly arrested for vagrancy—that is, wandering around without money or work and refusing to work. Those miners were forced to work for the companies for free. She heard of the guards who carried and fired machine guns at the miners.

The Forbes mining camp during the bitter 1913–1914 Colorado miners' strike.

In response to all she heard, Mother Jones told the miners and their wives to fight. "Fight like hell till you go to Heaven!" she told them. She encouraged the miners to work together to improve their lives, and she told them never to give up on the strike. "Rise up and strike. If you are too cowardly to fight, there are enough women in this country to come in and beat it out of you. If it is slavery or strike, why I say strike, until the last one of you drop into your graves."

The miners stuck with the strike, and no coal came out of the mines. The mining companies began to lose money. They needed a way to make the miners go back to work so they decided to scare the miners with a specially built armored automobile. They fitted the armored car with a machine gun that could shoot 400 times in one minute. They called it the Death Special.

Company guards took the Death Special to the tent colonies. During the first week of the strike, one guard walked up to a group of striking miners at the Forbes tent colony. The guard waved a white flag, which meant that he wanted a truce. He asked the group of miners if they were members of the union, and they answered that they were. Quickly the guard jumped to one side and warned them, "Look out for yourselves." Then company guards fired the machine gun on the group of striking miners. One striker was killed in the attack, and several more were wounded.

Mother Jones was appalled by the mining companies' cruel treatment of the striking miners. She led a group of 2,000 union members to see Governor Elias Ammons in Denver. The group of miners told the governor of the machine guns and the beatings.

93

Governor Ammons was scared by the power of the mining companies, and he did whatever he thought the companies wanted. A company employee even wrote his speeches. The governor denied that the company guards and the militia had behaved badly, and he said he needed proof before he could do anything to help the miners. Finally he was convinced to visit southern Colorado to investigate the miners' claims.

In October, Mother Jones went to Washington, D.C., where she met with President Woodrow Wilson to discuss the situation of Colorado miners. In November, she went to Boston and Washington to make speeches on the plight of miners.

Meanwhile, in late October, Governor Ammons had called in the state militia. At first the strikers thought the state militia had come to protect them from the company guards, and they welcomed the soldiers with flags and applause. Soon, however, the strikers realized that the militia meant to break their strike, no matter how much violence the soldiers had to use. In fact, some of the mine guards had enlisted in the state militia, and the coal company was paying part of the soldiers' wages.

This 1914 pro–Mother Jones cartoon is entitled "Justice in Colorado."

General John Chase, the man who was in charge of the militia, did not like Mother Jones. He said that Mother Jones was dangerous, claiming that she caused trouble by "inflaming the minds of the strikers." General Chase warned Mother Jones not to come back to the strike zone. He said publicly that if she came back, he would have her arrested.

It is no surprise that Mother Jones ignored the general's warnings. She did not like to be told what to do, and he did not scare her any more than the Baldwin-Felts guards or the local police did. She was much more worried about "her boys" and their families making it through the winter than she was about a general's threats against her. In December, the worst blizzard to hit Colorado in 30 years dumped snow on the mountains. The striking miners and their families huddled close together in their tents, trying to keep warm.

On January 4, 1914, Mother Jones returned to the strike zone and went to the town of Trinidad. There General Chase kept his word. His soldiers quickly arrested Mother Jones and drove her to the train station. Soldiers on horseback patrolled the streets to keep striking miners from interfering. Mother Jones was whisked away to Denver.

Governor Ammons supported the general's decision to remove Mother Jones from the strike zone. The governor claimed that three-fourths of the strike violence could be blamed on Mother Jones's speeches. Mother Jones pretended to go along with the governor's wishes. She stayed in Denver for eight days, talking with UMW officials and buying supplies and shoes for the strikers. But quietly she prepared to go back to Trinidad, for she had promised the striking miners she would return to them.

Mother Jones knew there were company detectives in the Denver train station. The detectives waited there to catch her if she tried to go back to the strike zone in the southern coalfields. So Mother Jones figured out a way to trick the detectives. On January 12, she sneaked aboard a train heading south, getting on before it pulled into the Denver station. The detectives, waiting in the station, never saw her. She smiled to herself as she took the southbound train to Trinidad.

Mother Jones knew that the militia would be watching for her at the train station in Trinidad. She made friends with the train's conductor and asked him to stop the train just before it got to Trinidad. She got off before the train pulled into town and walked the rest of the way. She arrived in Trinidad and had breakfast at the Toltec Hotel. But General Chase soon learned that she was in town, and he came himself to arrest her. One hundred and fifty soldiers on horseback appeared outside the hotel. General Chase and his soldiers arrested her in her hotel room during a meeting with a group of miners. The soldiers took her away as the miners watched in frightened astonishment.

The U.S. Constitution forbids the government from detaining or imprisoning citizens without formally charging them. That means the government must give a reason supported by some evidence or reliable information. Yet Mother Jones was the 28th person to be arrested without charges that week. She was taken to the Mount San Raphael Hospital, on the eastern edge of Trinidad. The hospital, which was run by nuns, had been made into a kind of jail during the strike. Mother Jones was kept in a single room, with a cot, a chair, and a table, for more than two months. She was not allowed to receive mail, newspapers, or visitors. The only person who saw her was the union lawyer. While she was kept prisoner in the hospital, she was heavily guarded. She described the big, uniformed militiamen who stood in the hall outside her door. The soldiers had "guns on their shoulders and a belt of bullets around their stomachs and a saber hanging to their sides."

The striking miners were furious that General Chase had arrested their "Mother." Angry people held local and national protests against her arrest. Women planned a march in Trinidad to protest the arrest of Mother Jones. The wives of the strikers called on other women to come to Trinidad. A thousand women—wives, mothers, and sisters of the striking miners—marched with their children down Commercial Street in Trinidad. The women carried banners reading, "God Bless Mother Jones" and "We're For Mother Jones." The women tried to carry one that read, "Has Governor Ammons Forgotten He Has a Mother?" but soldiers ordered them not to carry that banner.

During the march, General Chase tried to break up the group of women, but his frightened horse ran into a horse and buggy. He fell off his horse. The women burst out laughing, which deeply embarrassed the general. He got back on and angrily ordered his soldiers to ride their horses into the crowd. The women and children ran, screaming. Several women were cut by the soldiers' swords and knocked down by their horses.

General Chase called Mother Jones a "dangerous rabble-rouser." However, he did offer to release her if she promised to leave the strike area. Of course, she refused. The public continued to complain about her arrest. Finally, on March 16, after nine weeks alone in the hospital room, soldiers put Mother Jones on a train heading north to Denver. The soldiers rode on the train with her, and when they arrived in Denver, the soldiers took her to the Oxford Hotel. There they let her go.

In Denver, Mother Jones met again with Governor Ammons, who encouraged her not to return to the strike zone. Once again she ignored his advice, and on the night of March 22, she tried again to return to Trinidad by train.

Things had gotten worse in the strikers' tent colonies while Mother Jones had been detained. Armed guards surrounded the tents every night. They tore down the strikers' tents at will. The strikers and their families, nervous about what would happen next, dug holes underneath the tents. They thought they could hide in the holes with their children if they were attacked.

Somehow General Chase found out that Mother Jones was coming back. He even knew she was on the train headed for Trinidad. With the situation as menacing as it was, he did not want her to speak to the strikers, and he was not going to let her arrive in Trinidad again.

Early in the morning of March 23, 1914, the train carrying Mother Jones stopped in Walsenburg, a town north of Trinidad. Mother Jones was asleep when soldiers came on to look for her. Under orders from the governor, the soldiers took Mother Jones off the train and handed her over to the Walsenburg town sheriff. He locked her up in the Huerfano County Jail, where she was kept with again no charges brought against her.

Women in Trinidad, Colorado, protest Mother Jones's arrest.

This third arrest was

the worst. She was locked up in a dark cell in the basement of the jail. The cell was cold, damp, and full of rats. She slept in her clothes and fought off the rats with an empty beer bottle. No one was allowed to see or talk with her. Through a tiny window she could see people's feet as they passed by the jail. Crowds of people gathered around the jail. Once in a while children knelt by the window and waved to her, until the soldiers chased them away.

While she was in jail, she somehow managed to smuggle out a letter that told about the horrible things being done to the miners in Colorado. The open letter was read in many meetings of her supporters. It helped people across the United States to know what was going on in Colorado. She wrote: "In all my strike experiences I have seen no horrors equal to those perpetuated [done] by General Chase and his crops of Baldwin-Felts detectives. . . . I have only to close my eyes to see the hot tears of the orphans and the widows of working men, and hear the mourning of the broken hearts. . . ." Many people saw her letter. It helped gain public support for the striking miners, and it let people know that she was in jail. Many people felt sorry for Mother Jones and thought an old lady like her should not be kept in a cold basement jail. Finally, after 26 days, the sheriff released her. No charges had ever been made against her, and no one ever explained why she had been arrested.

Soon after she was released, she traveled once again to Washington, D.C. In April 1914, she testified to Congress about the lives of the striking miners. She told Congress about the violence and the armed company guards who beat and shot the miners. The guards, she said, were "permitted to arm themselves with machine guns and use them on the workers, because the ruling class wants quick results." Her testimony led to much public outcry in support of the Colorado miners.

While she was in Washington that April, something even more terrible happened in Colorado. It happened near Trinidad, at the Ludlow tent colony, the largest of the strikers' colonies. Two hundred strikers' tents had been set up there. About 1,200 people, speaking a variety of languages, lived in the organized community. The Ludlow tent colony had at its center a large meeting tent, which flew the American flag and also served as a place for church services. On April 20, 1914, the day after many of the mining families had celebrated Easter, soldiers surrounded the Ludlow tent colony. The miners and the soldiers each thought the other side was planning an attack.

Suddenly, at about nine in the morning, the soldiers fired their machine guns at the tents. People poured screaming and bleeding out of their tents. Many women and children fled into the hills. One little boy was shot in the head as he ran to his tent to save his kitten. One man, who tried to rescue women and children, was killed when a soldier brutally hit him on the head with a heavy rifle.

The strikers who had guns stayed hidden in the tent colony. They fired back on the soldiers. The fighting continued for hours. But by evening the strikers had run out of bullets. Some strikers joined their families in the hills above Ludlow. Other strikers and their families stayed in the tent colony, trying to hide in their tents. As night fell, the soldiers grew even more violent. They set the tents on fire and stole any property they wanted from the burning tents. The tents and everything that was left in them—including some strikers and their families—burned with an awful glow through the night.

No one knows for sure, but probably 32 people were shot or burned to death in what came to be called the Ludlow Massacre. Some of them burned to death as they hid in holes dug under their tents. Under one tent, the burned bodies of 11 children and 2 women were found. Twenty-four-year-old Mary Petrucci lost all three of her children in the fire.

The Ludlow Massacre pushed the striking miners over the emotional edge. Their families and friends had been killed. Everything they had owned was burned up in their tents. The miners were so angry that they forgot their fear and began to fight against the company guards and soldiers. They got guns and took over towns and mines around Ludlow, setting fire to company buildings. Other people who were angry about the massacre helped the miners. For 10 days the miners and their helpers burned and destroyed anything connected with the mining companies.

The miners attacked state militia soldiers who tried to stop

99

them and drove the frightened soldiers out of Trinidad. News of the fights and destruction spread across the country. Within days demonstrations and protest rallies supporting the miners were held in Denver, San Francisco, Chicago, New York, and other cities. People demanded that President Woodrow Wilson send the U.S. Army into Colorado. President Wilson knew he had to stop the violence, and he decided to send U.S. cavalry troops into Colorado to replace the militia soldiers. On April 29, 1914, the first 175 federal soldiers arrived in Denver. The fighting was over—but not the strike.

The Ludlow Massacre and the strikers' response brought much attention to mining in Colorado. People began to ask hard questions about the mining companies. They wondered what could have caused so much violence and destruction.

John D. Rockefeller, Jr., blamed Mother Jones for the strikes and the violence. He and the other mine owners thought that her speeches against them had convinced the miners to fight back. In a pamphlet published by Rockefeller, General Chase wrote, "I confidently believe that most of the murders and other acts of violent crime committed in the strike region have been inspired by this woman's incendiary utterances."

Mother Jones traveled around the country, ignoring Chase's accusations. She spoke out against the horrible things that had happened at Ludlow. Soon after the Ludlow Massacre, she spoke to a meeting of the United Mine Workers in Kansas:

> You see, my brothers, the trouble with us all is we don't feel the pains of our fellow beings in the great struggle. I wonder if the nation felt the horror of that affair at Ludlow? Why, if that happened in Mexico we would go down to clean up Mexico, and it happened here at home and there is very little said about it, when every man should shoulder his gun and start to Colorado to stop the war there. . . . No time in modern history has there been anything so horrible as this trouble in Colorado.

Mother Jones went to Washington again. She told Congress

that the mines should be taken over by the federal government. In October, she visited President Wilson and warned him that the Colorado state government could not keep the situation from getting violent again. She urged him to keep federal soldiers in the area. President Wilson sent a group of people called a federal commission to Colorado. The commission, trying to settle the strike, suggested a three-year truce and the rehiring of all miners who had not broken the law. The settlement would not include union recognition or pay raises. The system of mine guards would end, and the state labor laws were supposed to be enforced. The leaders of the UMW, which was ready to end the strike, accepted the commission's suggestion. But then the mining companies refused to accept the commission's suggestion. They refused to give in even a little. So the strike continued.

The strike dragged on for a total of 15 months. It was finally ended when President Wilson set up a settlement committee in December 1914 and the UMW called off the strike. The strike had cost the UMW $4 million and had not won anything better for

Mother Jones gave speeches and led parades to support the Colorado miners' strike of 1913–1914.

the miners, whose lives were basically the same as before the strike. In fact, there was still no way to make the state enforce its labor laws. Sixty-five people had been killed, including 43 women and children.

After the strike, the miners received more national attention than ever before. The federal government wrote reports on the conditions in the mines, blaming the mining companies for poor working conditions. The government said that the mining companies needed to improve the lives of the miners. But to prevent the regular unions from coming into the mining towns, the mining companies created company unions, where miners were represented but decisions were still controlled by the companies.

In 1912, Congress had passed a new law creating the U.S. Commission on Industrial Relations, to investigate labor conditions. In 1915, President Woodrow Wilson asked the group to find out why there had been so much violence around the mines. Later that spring of 1915, Mother Jones spoke to the commission. She told what had happened at Ludlow, strongly condemning the mining companies who had encouraged such violence. She suggested that the government take the coal mines away from private companies and remove armed guards and detectives from strike zones. She tried to help the commission understand the strikers. She thought people in power could not understand how workers lived. "I feel that men in that position do not grasp these things as they are, nor do the people outside, nor do our officials who live in offices, nor do our newspaper men," she said. "It takes those who are down with them to see the horrors of this industrial tragedy that is going on in our nation today."

Mother Jones leads a march commemorating the Ludlow Massacre of 1914.

After the failure of the strike in Colorado, Mother Jones was involved in many smaller strikes all around the country and even in British Columbia in western Canada. In 1915, she made speeches and campaigned for several political candidates. She spent time with the striking streetcar workers in El Paso, Texas, and New York City. Always she encouraged the workers to fight for their rights. With her unfailing optimism, she told them not to give up and not to be afraid. She always believed that justice would win.

In 1916, Congress passed another national child labor law. But like the earlier one, it was overturned by the courts. However, a 1916 law dealing with railroad workers was upheld by the Supreme Court. It gave railroad workers an eight-hour workday with extra pay for overtime work.

In 1917, Mother Jones spent most of her time in West Virginia with the coal miners. She spoke out against World War I, which was going on in Europe. She hoped that U.S. workers would not be sent to fight. But when the United States declared war and entered into World War I in April of that year, Mother Jones changed her mind about the war. Now she saw it as a fight for democracy and as a chance for U.S. workers to gain more respect and greater power at home.

Although about 112,000 American soldiers and sailors died in battle or from influenza or pneumonia, the war brought more production of goods and more employment in the United States. The government tried to maintain industrial peace at home during the war by encouraging companies to recognize unions and by urging workers not to strike. With this government support, many workers won higher wages. Mother Jones saw how working conditions and wages improved as the miners were considered important citizens in the war effort. The coal they dug was used to run factories. The metals they mined were used to build weapons and ships.

Mother Jones began to talk about her love for Uncle Sam. She told workers to buy war bonds, which helped to pay for the war, and she encouraged miners to work hard to produce coal and metals for the war effort. She rode at the front of a "Win the War" parade through Charleston, West Virginia. In the car with her were the mayor and the county sheriff, and behind her was a mile-long procession of union miners.

In 1918 and 1919, she worked to organize steelworkers in Pennsylvania and Ohio. Steel was one of the few industries that did not greatly improve labor conditions during the war. After the war ended in 1918, conditions grew even worse as employers tried to prevent strikes and take back the few gains that the workers had managed to achieve during the war.

Steelworkers still worked 12-hour days and 7-day weeks beside very hot, loud furnaces. Because many of them were immigrants from other countries and spoke little English, they were difficult to organize into unions and found it hard to speak out for their rights. Steel companies had been able to convince judges to issue injunctions forbidding public speeches by union organizers. Ignoring or avoiding the court injunctions, Mother Jones visited steel towns, holding meetings and making speeches. In her speeches, Mother Jones said that the steel company owners had stomachs and hearts and tears made of steel. She encouraged the steelworkers to join the union and work against the cruel company owners. Her speeches were very well attended. Even the immigrant steelworkers came to listen to her. Although many of them could not understand her, they could feel the emotion in her words. She claimed to be more than 80 years old, and people were amazed at her great energy and enthusiasm.

Sometimes there were injunctions against speaking in towns near the Pennsylvania border. So she would hold her meetings just across the border in Ohio. Mother Jones was arrested several times for breaking the injunctions against public speeches. Once, when she was speaking from inside a car, police pulled her out and arrested her.

The steelworkers were getting tired of their long hours and bad treatment. Finally, the organized workers could wait no longer. On September 22, 1919, the union voted to go on strike. Half of all the steelworkers in the country walked out. In response, the steel companies clamped down. The companies convinced local judges to issue tougher injunctions. Now all meetings, public or private, were outlawed. Any group of three or four men could be arrested on suspicion of meeting to discuss the strike. In cities across the United States striking steelworkers were attacked and beaten.

The steel companies tried to make the strikers look bad by claiming that the strike was part of a radical foreign plot. They claimed that the strike had been organized by the Soviet Union. In 1917 there had been a workers' revolution against the Russian emperor, who was called the czar, and the country's name was later changed to the Soviet Union. The Communist party did away with private property, and the Soviet government became the owner of the factories. Communist revolutionaries were called Reds. Many Americans, especially those who owned factories or other property, thought these Reds had dangerous ideas that might spread to the United States.

The steel companies claimed that the Communists in the Soviet Union were trying to take over the United States and were sending secret agents to the United States to help start a revolution like the one in Russia. People grew scared. The fear that the steel companies helped to spread was called the Red Scare. The Red Scare, which peaked in 1919 and 1920, helped turn public opinion against the striking steelworkers.

Newspapers accused Mother Jones of being a Communist revolutionary. The police in many areas found ways to stop her from talking to anyone. Even if she spoke to one man in public, police arrested Mother Jones for "unlawful assembly." Even if she stopped to talk to a woman on the street about her child, guards on horseback would chase her away. But she continued to speak out. After being refused the right to speak to steelworkers in a park in Gary, Indiana, Mother Jones was able to address them in a local auditorium. The building was, however, surrounded by armed federal soldiers to prevent violence.

By the beginning of 1920, the steel strike had been broken. But Mother Jones was sure that someday, the steelworkers would get justice. "Injustice boils in men's hearts, as does steel in its cauldron," she said, "ready to pour forth, white hot, in the fullness of time."

In 1920, she went back to West Virginia. She went to help the last non-union area in the south of the state. Miners in southern

West Virginia still lived a very poor and hard life. They had no unions and were completely controlled by the coal companies. Workers were still paid in scrip and had to use it in company stores. Coal miners had begun strikes in 1919. The company-hired gunmen were soon fighting the coal miners in violent battles such as the one in the town of Matewan in May 1920.

That August, Mother Jones held a meeting in Princeton, West Virginia. It was the first labor meeting ever held there. Six or seven thousand people came to see her. So did several truckloads of Baldwin-Felts detectives. After the meeting, she feared that the detectives would follow her and murder her. She bravely left the meeting, heading toward the place where she was staying and fooling the detectives by taking a wrong turn.

In 1921, she left West Virginia for a period, traveling to Mexico to address the Pan-American Federation of Labor. This organization tried to protect workers throughout both North and South America. Mother Jones was the guest of the Mexican government, since the revolutionaries she had helped 10 years earlier were now members of the government. The Mexican people were excited to see her, and they crowded around her arriving train, forcing it to stop on the tracks. They greeted her by throwing red and blue flowers all around her. Mother Jones had won a special place in the hearts of Mexican workers. She was given a government car and chauffeur to use during her visit. She visited a coal miners' strike, where she saw the same poor conditions that miners faced in the United States. Mother Jones enjoyed her time in Mexico. She was full of energy and cheer, and she happily went sight-seeing. Everywhere she went she was greeted with joy by Mexican workers. She was a hero to them.

On January 13, 1921, she gave a speech to the Pan-American Federation of Labor. She said she belonged to no one union. She belonged, she said, to workers wherever they were in "slavery." "I speak so much about the miners, because mining is the basic industry and the miners are the federated army in the labor movement in America." With "her boys" always on her mind, she could not stay forever in Mexico.

She went back to West Virginia during the summer of 1921. Bloody, violent fights had broken out in Logan County between the mine operators and the miners. The miners were fighting to get the armed guards removed from the mines. Mother Jones tried to calm the miners. Believing that the fighting would not help the miners and would only lead to unnecessary deaths, she discouraged them from fighting. She told them of a telegram from President Warren G. Harding, which promised that the President would help remove the armed guards. Other union officials did not believe that the President had sent a telegram. They called Washington, D.C., and found out that the President had not sent a telegram to the miners. Mother Jones had made up the telegram and lied about it because she wanted to stop the miners from going ahead with a bloody fight. Her lie cost her respect among many union miners. She was called a "traitor," and she left West Virginia in embarrassment.

As she was leaving, a vicious battle broke out between the guards and the striking miners. President Harding feared the battle would turn into a civil war. On August 30, he placed the entire state of West Virginia under martial law and ordered the miners to stop fighting and go home. But the miners ignored the President's order. As the fighting worsened, the President decided to use force to end the battle between the coal miners, who now numbered as many as 20,000, and the company guards. On September 1, he sent 2,500 federal soldiers and 14 bombing planes to West Virginia. The fierce fight that followed was called the Battle of Blair Mountain, and it lasted for two days. It was the largest armed conflict in the history of American labor. Thousands of men fought on both sides, and there were many men killed and wounded.

The government used machine guns and tear gas against the strikers, and finally the strikers realized they could not win against these government weapons. On September 4, 1921, they surrendered, and the strike was ended. The total number of miners killed in the fighting has never been known, but 500 strik were arrested and charged with treason and murder. The rest the strikers went back to the same poor working conditio against which they had been fighting.

CHAPTER ELEVEN

Mother Jones: Lessons from Her Life

After 1922, Mother Jones's health began to fail. She had to go into the hospital several times. She had rheumatism, which swelled her joints and slowed her down with pain. For two weeks in August 1922, she needed constant nursing, and many people were afraid she would die. Her hands were so swollen with rheumatism that she could not hold a spoon. By the end of September, however, she felt much better. From this time on though, she had trouble walking and was often weak. She suffered on and off from pain in her knees. For these problems her doctor told her to drink a little whiskey.

She began to go deaf and slowly lost some of her eyesight. Despite her health problems, she still managed to participate in several strikes. She also visited friends and political leaders and gave speeches.

Many times people had urged Mother Jones to write her autobiography, the story of her life. In the spring and summer of 1924, she did just that. She went back to Chicago, where she worked on her autobiography with a Socialist journalist named Mary Field Parton. Mary Parton had written articles for several labor magazines. Probably, Parton took notes while Mother Jones talked about her life. Mother Jones was hoping to use the money from the sales of her book to help defend union men who were accused of crimes.

After several months of work, Mother Jones grew tired of writing. She was ready to do something else. Perhaps she found it more difficult to remember events accurately. Her autobiography, which was printed in 1925, is filled with misspelled names and incorrect dates. Although it is not completely accurate, her book shows the strength of her passion to support workers in their struggle for a better life.

While she was in Chicago, dressmakers there went on strike.

During the five months of the strike, more than 1,500 workers were arrested. Mother Jones was there to encourage them and to visit them at strike meetings. This was her last active participation in a strike.

But the labor movement suffered greatly in the late 1920s. Unions lost membership, while industry gained strength. Across the country, unemployment went down, and average wages went up. (In the coal industry, however, workers' earnings peaked between 1923 and 1925, and then steadily declined.) There were still many poor and unhappy workers, but the national economy was just strong enough to prevent most workers from feeling the desperation that would lead them to strike. As they grew stronger, employers practiced "union busting," or breaking up unions. The Wobblies, who had been strong until World War I, were no longer active, and the Socialist party lost strength. Both the Wobblies and the Socialists were victims of the Red Scare because their ideas were said to be too revolutionary for the United States.

Mother Jones grew sad. She realized that conditions for "her boys" were getting worse instead of better. "All the world's history has produced no more brutal and savage times than these," she said, "and this nation will perish [die] if we do not change these conditions."

She spent more and more time in bed. In 1928, she moved to Hyattsville, Maryland, home of Walter and Lillie Mae Burgess. Walter Burgess was a retired coal miner who had known Mother Jones for a long time. He knew that Mother Jones could not take care of herself, so he offered her a place to stay.

Mother Jones's weakness did not keep her from planning a big event. Whether or not it was really the date of her birth, she celebrated her one-hundredth birthday on May 1, 1930. For years she had planned to go back to Chicago for the special day, but now her failing health kept her from making the trip. Instead, friends, union leaders, and reporters gathered with her at the Burgesses' home in Maryland. It was a warm, sunny day. Mother Jones managed to get out of bed for a few hours. Wearing a new black silk dress, she was carried downstairs and outside. She sat in a rocking chair under an apple tree. Happily, she greeted the many guests who had come to congratulate her on her birthday.

She was given a huge five-layered birthday cake, with one hundred lighted candles, donated by the local bakers' union. Sitting in her chair, with a blanket over her lap, she sliced into the cake and shared it with her many friends and well-wishers. The flowers and many birthday gifts she received covered the lawn. An orchestra played and food was spread on several tables.

Mother Jones said we "have only one journey to go through life; let us do the best we can for humanity . . .while we are here."

Paramount News sent a movie crew to film her. She was very excited, for she had only seen a "talkie" once in her life. Talking to the movie camera, she told workers to "stick together and be loyal to one another." Her voice was clear and strong. There were newspaper reporters, too. To a *New York Times* reporter, she said, "I wouldn't trade what I've done for what John D. Rockefeller has done. I've done the best I could to make the world a better place for poor, hard-working people."

During the party in Maryland, she was visited by a group of poor workers who walked from Washington, D.C., to see her. The stock market had crashed in late 1929, and by 1930 the Great Depression was beginning to affect the whole country. Businesses were failing and unemployment was rising. By camping in the U.S. capital, the workers hoped to get the government to pay attention to their problems. The group marched the eight miles out to Hyattsville to honor a woman who spent her whole life helping workers.

Still following the actions of the labor movement, still hoping for justice for working people, Mother Jones died on Sunday, November 30, 1930. In the midst of the Great Depression, her death was deeply mourned. Thousands of people came to see Mother Jones's body. The casket that held her body was surrounded with many flowers, burning candles, and the banners of the miners' unions. People passed by quietly and sadly. Thousands more came to Mother Jones's funeral on December 8. She was buried in a UMW cemetery in Mt. Olive, Illinois. She had asked to be buried there, in the only union-owned cemetery in the United States.

As they mourned her death, people remembered what she had done with her life. In a speech to striking miners in West Virginia, Mother Jones had once said the following:

> Now, I want to say, my friends, I have only one journey to go through this life; you have only one journey to go through this life; let us all do the best we can for humanity, for mankind, while we are here. That is my mission, to do what I can to raise mankind to break his chains.

All her life, Mother Jones wanted working people to have better lives. She wanted shorter workdays, so that workers would have a chance to read and to think. She wanted children to go to school instead of working in factories or mills. She wanted owners of industry to share with workers the great wealth that comes from industry. "My life work," she had said in 1912, "has been to try to educate the worker to a sense of the wrongs he has had to suffer, and does suffer—and to stir up the oppressed to a point of getting off their knees and demanding that which I believe to be rightfully theirs."

After her shop burned in Chicago back in 1871, Mother Jones never had a home. She once told Congress that her address was like her shoes—it traveled with her. When she was asked where she lived, Mother Jones answered: "I will tell you. I live wherever there is a bunch of workers fighting the robber. My home is with the workers."

She moved from place to place, staying in people's homes whenever possible. She carried all her possessions with her in a little bundle. She never saved money, giving it instead to workers in need. She did not trust banks. Whenever she had extra money, she gave it to friends to keep for her. Mother Jones never held a steady job for long, so she often had to borrow money to live on. She never paid taxes. She just did not worry about herself; instead, she went wherever she thought she was needed.

Mother Jones believed in right and wrong. Her idea of what was right might change from one situation to the next. For example, she usually spoke out against violence. But in one West Virginia strike, she encouraged the miners to buy guns and fight back against the company guards. She did not like to compromise. She was not scared of jails or guns. "No Gatling guns, no militia, no courts, have ever intimidated me," she said. To a crowd of West Virginia miners, Mother Jones once claimed, "I am not afraid of jails. We build the jails, and when we get ready we will put them behind the bars. That may happen very soon— things happen overnight." Mother Jones did many things that most women of her day would not do. She was a labor organizer, working all day and night with men. She drank and she swore. She spent time in jail. She traveled a great deal, in a time when travel was much more difficult and time-consuming than it is today.

In her lifetime, she insulted many people, calling the U.S. Senate a "house of thieves" and rich industrialists "high-class burglars." She spoke out against churches and politicians. She made enemies with her sharp tongue. Her enemies tried to hurt her by accusing her of bad behavior in her earlier days. Many people heard this accusation, but few believed it.

She once spoke to a group of women in New York who were working to help get women the right to vote. She told them that they must stand up for free speech. How could they, asked one woman, when they did not have the right to vote? Mother Jones responded, "I have never had a vote and I have raised hell all over this country! You don't need a vote to raise hell! You need convictions and a voice!"

With convictions and a voice, and very little else, Mary Harris "Mother" Jones spent her life with working people. Wherever workers needed encouragement and support, she went. She was with strikers in textile strikes, in streetcar strikes, and in railroad strikes. She was there with them in silk mill strikes, in shirtwaist strikes, in ironworker strikes, and in coal mine strikes.

She claimed to have met every President since Lincoln. She was watched and reported on by U.S. military spies. Once she visited a West Virginia man who was in jail for stealing a pair of shoes. She told him, "What a shame. If you had stolen a railroad they would have made you a United States Senator."

While she was still alive, writers and reporters predicted that Mother Jones would come to be known as a very famous labor leader after her death. Their prediction has not come true. Perhaps one of the reasons why Mother Jones did not become known as a famous leader after her death is that very few details of her life were written down. She was loved by poor people, many of whom did not know how to write, and most of her speeches were not recorded. Only a small number of her speeches and writings have survived.

Upon her death, an anonymous poet wrote about Mother Jones. The poem was put to music and sung in the mountains of West Virginia:

The world today is mourning
The death of Mother Jones;
Grief and sorrow hover
Over the miners' homes;
This grand old champion of labor
Has gone to a better land,
But the hard-working miners,
They miss her guiding hand.

Through the hills and over the valleys,
In every mining town,
Mother Jones was ready to help them—
She never turned them down.
In front with the striking miners
She always could be found,
She fought for right and justice,
She took a noble stand.

With a spirit strong and fearless
She hated that which was wrong;
She never gave up fighting
Until her breath was gone.
May the workers all get together
To carry out her plan,
And bring back better conditions
To every laboring man.

Mother Jones had many enemies. The rich industrialists did not like her. Some union officials did not like her, for she was not afraid to disagree with them in public.

She knew that she had enemies, but she did not mind. She was glad that she said things that made people angry. She was glad that she caused trouble. She knew that she said what she thought was right. She always stood up for what she believed. That was why the workers loved Mother Jones.

1830-44	Sometime in this period Mary Harris is born in Ireland.
1840s	Mary and her mother and two brothers join her father in the United States and they move to Canada.
1858-59	Mary attends Toronto Normal School.
1859-60	Mary teaches school in Monroe, Michigan.
1860-61	Mary Harris runs a dressmaking business in Chicago, Illinois.
1861	Mary Harris marries George Jones while teaching in Memphis, Tennessee.
1867	George Jones and the Joneses' children die in the yellow fever epidemic. Mary Harris Jones returns to dressmaking in Chicago.
1871	The Great Chicago Fire destroys Jones's shop and everything she has. She begins to work with the Knights of Labor.
1877	Jones is involved in railroad strikes in northeastern United States.
1894	Jones is involved in a coal miners' strike in Birmingham, Alabama. She works in Southern cotton mills, learning about the terrible conditions suffered by child workers.
1895	Jones helps found a weekly newspaper called *Appeal to Reason*. She travels, selling subscriptions and investigating the conditions of workers.
1897	Jones attends the founding of the Social Democracy of America. She organizes striking miners in West Virginia and Pennsylvania.

1899	Jones leads wives of miners on a march at the Drip Mouth mine in Arnot, Pennsylvania.
1900-1902	A paid organizer for the United Mine Workers, Jones organizes miners and families in West Virginia. She is arrested and jailed several times.
1903	Jones leads the "Crusade of the Mill Children" from Philadelphia to New York.
1903-1904	Jones helps organize coal miners in Colorado. She leaves the UMW and works for the Western Federation of Miners. She is deported by the governor of Colorado and quarantined in Utah.
1905	Jones helps found the Industrial Workers of the World.
1907-11	Jones works to raise money for Mexican revolutionaries. She helps the women of Greensburg, Pennsylvania, sing themselves out of jail.
1910	Jones organizes brewery workers in Milwaukee, Wisconsin.
1912-13	Jones works at the Paint Creek–Cabin Creek strike in West Virginia. She is arrested and released after national outcry.
1913-14	Miners go on strike in the north and south of Colorado. Jones is repeatedly detained in Trinidad. She speaks out after the Ludlow Massacre.
1915	Jones meets with Rockefeller and speaks to the Commission on Industrial Relations. She works with miners, garment workers, and streetcar workers.
1917-21	Jones works on and off with coal miners in West Virginia. She supports a major steelworkers' strike in Pennsylvania and Ohio and coal miners' strikes in West Virginia.

1921	Jones visits Mexico for Pan-American Federation of Labor Congress, where she is welcomed as a hero.
1924	Jones writes her autobiography in Chicago. While there, she is involved in a dressmakers' strike.
1922-1930	Jones spends most of her time in retirement near Washington, D.C. She celebrates her 100th birthday on May 1, 1930.
1930	Jones dies on November 30, near Hyattsville, Maryland.

anarchism A political theory and philosophy whose central belief is that people can live justly and happily together without government. Anarchists favor a society based on voluntary cooperation. Some anarchists believe that violence and revolutionary action are needed to overthrow organized government by force.

bail Money paid by the accused to gain his or her release from prison in the period before trial to make sure he or she will show up for the trial. If the accused person does not show up for the trial, he or she loses the money.

blacklist To put on a list of people who are disapproved of or people who are to be punished or boycotted. Employers sometimes passed around to other employers a list of workers to be refused work because they had joined a union or held opinions an employer didn't like.

boycott To refuse to have anything to do with the products or services of an employer in order to force the employer to accept certain conditions that the union wants.

breakers The equipment and place where coal is crushed, sorted, and cleaned.

capitalism An economic system in which individuals or corporations own the industries and businesses. Under capitalism, the prices, production, and distribution of goods are determined mainly by the free market and not by means of government control.

checkweighman A person employed by miners or unions to check the weighing of coal or ore by a company weigher.

coalfield A region in which there are deposits of coal.

collective bargaining The negotiation of an agreement between an employer or group of employers on one side and a union or group of unions on the other. Agreements reached usually deal with wages, hours of work, work benefits, and working conditions.

company town A community that is dependent upon one company for all or most of its needed activities and services such as work, housing, stores, and government. The company usually owns the stores, buildings, and land in the town.

company union A labor union made up of workers of a single company and controlled by that company. Company unions are not connected with a larger labor organization or a national group.

cribbing A framework added by coal companies to a railroad car so that it could hold more coal. For coal miners who were paid by the carload, this meant filling a larger space but not being paid more for the extra coal mined.

depression A period of reduced factory production, widespread unemployment and business failures, and a low level of construction and investment.

double-header Extra-long trains pulled by two engines.

foundry A building or business where metals such as iron are melted and poured into molds to make items such as tools.

general strike The stopping of work in many industries and places throughout a country in order to force employers or the government to meet certain demands.

injunction A court order prohibiting someone from doing something or commanding someone to undo some wrong or injury.

lockout The withholding of work by an employer and the closing of the business or factory in order to force the regular workers to give in to the employer's demands such as ending a strike.

martial law   The law and government run by military forces during times of emergency when the civilian law enforcement agencies (such as the police) are unable to maintain public order and safety.

militia   The citizens of a state who serve as a military force in times of emergency. These temporary citizen soldiers are not usually part of the regular army.

mine shaft   The tunnel leading down to where the coal or ore is mined.

open letter   A letter of protest or appeal usually addressed to an individual but really intended for the general public and often printed in a newspaper or magazine.

picket line   A line of workers organized by a union outside a workplace affected by a strike. The workers on the picket line try to convince those going in or out to join the strike. Picket lines are also used to publicize a labor dispute, to convince customers not to do business with the company, or to show the union's desire to represent the workers.

pluck-me store   A company store from which workers were often required to buy their groceries and other items. Sometimes the company paid its workers in scrip that could only be spent in the company store, which would overcharge its customers.

relief   Help for the poor in the form of money or goods.

scab   A person who takes the place of a worker who is on strike. People who work for wages lower than the wages approved of by a labor union are also called scabs.

scrip   A form of payment in company paper "money" instead of U.S. money, which the worker could spend at the company store or for other company-owned services in a company town.

short-weighting   Weighing on scales to show less than the true weight in order to cheat the miner who was paid by the weight of the coal mined.

socialism   An economic system in which private property and the distribution of income are under the people's control rather than determined by individuals following their own interests or by companies seeking private profit. In some socialist systems, all industries and private property are owned by the government; in others, only the largest and most important industries, banks, and natural resources are owned by the government.

solidarity   The sharing of common interests, objectives, and responsibilities.

strike   To stop working in order to force an employer to agree to some demand.

strikebreaker   A person hired to replace a striking worker. Striking workers will probably call such a person a scab; employers may call strikebreakers replacement workers.

sweatshop   A small factory or shop whose workers work long hours at low wages and under unhealthy conditions.

union   An organization of workers formed for the purpose of negotiating with employers on matters of wages, hours of work, working conditions, and work benefits.

union recognition   The official acceptance of a union by an employer. The employer accepts the union as the official representative of and bargainer for the workers.

vagrancy   The act of going about from place to place without money or a legal job but at the same time refusing to work although able to work.

BIBLIOGRAPHY

and Recommended Readings

American Social History Project. Who Built America? Working People and the Nation's Economy, Politics, Culture, and Society. Vol. 2: *From the Gilded Age to the Present.* New York: Pantheon, 1992.

*Atkinson, Linda. *Mother Jones: The Most Dangerous Woman in America.* New York: Crown Publishers, Inc. 1978.

Barbee, David Rankin. "Mother Jones Approaches a Century." *The Sunday Sun,* April 27, 1930, Magazine Section, 1.

Bird, Stewart, Dan Georgakas, and Deborah Shaffer. *Solidarity Forever: An Oral History of the IWW.* Chicago: Lake View Press, 1985.

Corbin, David Alan. *Life, Work, and Rebellion in the Coal Fields: The Southern West Virginia Miners, 1880-1922.* Urbana: University of Illinois Press, 1981.

Dubofsky, Melvyn. *"Big Bill" Haywood.* New York: St. Martin's Press, 1987.

Fetherling, Dale. *Mother Jones: The Miners' Angel.* Carbondale: Southern Illinois University Press, 1974.

Foner, Philip S., ed. *Mother Jones Speaks: Collected Writings and Speeches.* New York: Monad Press, 1983.

Knight, Harold V. *Working in Colorado: A Brief History of the Colorado Labor Movement.* Boulder, Colorado: University of Colorado, Center for Labor Education and Research, 1971.

*Levy, Elizabeth, and Tad Richards. *Struggle and Lose, Struggle and Win: The United Mine Workers.* New York: Four Winds Press, 1977.

Long, Priscilla. *Mother Jones: Woman Organizer.* Boston: South End Press, 1976.

——.*Where the Sun Never Shines: A History of America's Bloody Coal Industry.* New York: Paragon House, 1989.

——."The Voice of the Gun: Colorado's Great Coalfield War of

1913-1914." *Labor's Heritage* 1 (1989) 4-23.

McGovern, George S., and Leonard F. Guttridge. *The Great Coalfield War.* Boston: Houghton Mifflin, 1972.

Niles, Judith. *Seven Women: Portraits from the American Radical Tradition.* New York: The Viking Press, 1977.

Parton, Mary Field, ed. *The Autobiography of Mother Jones.* Chicago: Charles H. Kerr Publishing Company, 1980.

Schofield, Ann. "Mother Jones in Kansas: An Archival Note." *Labor History* 27 (1986): 431–42.

Steel, Edward M., ed. *The Correspondence of Mother Jones.* Pittsburgh: University of Pittsburgh Press, 1985.

——, ed. *The Speeches and Writings of Mother Jones.* Pittsburgh: University of Pittsburgh Press, 1988.

*Werstein, Irving. *Labor's Defiant Lady: The Story of Mother Jones.* New York: Thomas Y. Crowell Company, 1969.

*Especially recommended for younger readers.

Beckley, West Virginia

- Beckley Exhibition Coal Mine at New River Park, Adair Street, Beckley. Tours on battery–powered cars through a southern West Virginia coal mine, which operated from the 1890s to 1911. Also tours of a coal company house, lived in by miners from the 1920s to 1940s. Coal museum has examples of miners' hand tools and company scrip.

Mt. Olive, Illinois

- Mother Jones Memorial at the United Mine Workers Cemetery. The large granite monument was erected by the Progressive Miners and dedicated on October 11, 1936.

Trinidad, Colorado

- Ludlow Monument (12 miles northwest of Trinidad; take Interstate 15 north from Trinidad to the Ludlow exit). A granite monument has been erected by the United Mine Workers in com-memoration of the Ludlow Massacre.

Walsenburg, Colorado

- Walsenburg Mining Museum. Photographs and equipment used by miners and a simulated coal mine shaft.

INDEX

Joan C. Hawxhurst is a writer and editor living in Boulder, Colorado. She graduated from Virginia Tech and received an M.A. in international relations from Yale University. She has written several books for adolescents, as well as articles for newspapers and magazines. She also serves as editor of a newsletter for inter-faith families.

James P. Shenton is Professor of History at Columbia University. He has taught American History since 1951. Among his publications are *Robert John Walker, A Politician from Jackson to Lincoln*; *An Historian's History of the United States*, and *The Melting Pot*. Professor Shenton is a consultant to the National Endowment for the Humanities and has received the Mark Van Doren and Society of Columbia Graduates' Great Teachers Awards. He also serves as a consultant for CBS, NBC, and ABC educational programs.

COVER ILLUSTRATION
Gary McElhaney

MAPS
Go Media, Inc.

PHOTOGRAPHY CREDITS
p.6 The West Virginia and Regional History Collection, West Virginia University; p.10 BBC Hulton Picture Library; p.11 The Library of Congress; p.15 The West Virginia and Regional History Collection, West Virginia University; p.18 The Bettmann Archive; p.21 The Bettmann Archive; p.24 The Bettmann Archive; p.26 The Bettmann Archive; p.28 Brown Brothers; p.33 Brown Brothers; p.35 The Bettmann Archive; p.37 The Bettmann Archive; p.38 The Bettmann Archive; p.41 The Bettmann Archive; p.46 The Bettmann Archive; p.53 Brown Brothers; p.54 Culver Pictures; p.57 The Bettmann Archive; p.62 Colorado Historical Society; p.67 Colorado Historical Society; p.74 Brown Brothers; p.76 Culver Pictures; p.81 The West Virginia and Regional History Collection, West Virginia University; p.93 Library of Congress; p.94 The Denver Public Library, Western History Department; p.97 The Denver Public Library, Western History Department; p.101 Colorado Historical Society; p.102 Brown Brothers; p.110 West Virginia and Regional History Collection, West Virginia University.